boundblessings

A DEVOTIONAL

Madison Bloker

Printed in the United States of America.

ISBN 978-1-387-45577-5

Written by Madison Bloker.
Design by Madison Bloker.

www.boundblessings.com

boundblessings

TABLE OF CONTENTS

Bound Blessings is a devotional filled with an assortment of write-ups on seven different subjects. Subjects include faith, love, beauty, confidence, perseverance, positivity, and radiance. For each subject, there are twenty-one write-ups. This is because of the saying "it takes twenty-one days to form a habit." The hope is that this book will guide you to improve upon these subjects and also provide some light in your life. The goal of the book is to inspire, uplift, and enlighten, and to raise money for the University of Iowa Stead Family Children's Hospital through Wartburg College Dance Marathon. Check out www.boundblessings.com to see more of my writing and learn more about me!

faith

when good things fall apart

Sometimes good things will fall apart so better things can come together. God doesn't close a door without opening another.

Trusting in God means that you know He has the best plan for your life.

Disappointments are God's way of saying there is something better. Your situation may not be changing because God wants your heart to change first.

Rejection is redirection.

When God pushes you, He will either catch you or teach you how to fly.

If you no longer have someone you didn't think you'd ever lose, imagine the person God will give you that you never thought of having.

If a job fell through, imagine the better opportunity coming your way.

See the light, not the dark.

Things will get better. God knows what's best.

VERSE: Isaiah 40:31 "But those who trust in the Lord for help will find their strength renewed. They will rise on wings like eagles, they will run and not get weary; they will walk and not grow weak."

have faith in others

Have you ever had to work with somebody who just needed to take control of everything? They put a lot of pressure on themselves and didn't allow others to contribute with their full potential.

Don't be one of those people.
Learn to have faith in others.

Make it a point to see the good in all people, and highlight that good by giving people a chance. Set them up in a place where they can shine.

The best thing you can do is to get those around you to shine.

Lighten them up. Trust in them, and don't look for the bad right away. Don't complain when they don't have a specific talent you do or when they maybe do things differently.

Find out their gifts, and put them in places where they can share and fully utilize these gifts. Try not to get so frustrated when they don't do things your way. You'll often find your eyes opened to even better ways when you allow others to show theirs.

Believe in others.
Give others a chance.
Have faith.

VERSE: 1 Thessalonians 5:11 "Therefore encourage one another and build one another up, just as you are doing."

you are being guided

In life, we always want answers.

We're always looking to what's ahead, to what's coming next. We plan, we schedule, we fret about what we have to follow on the agenda. Sometimes it's almost as if we think we can see into the future.

News flash: you can't.

No matter how much scheduling or worrying you do, not everything goes according to plan.

Understand that there are unexpected twists and turns in life. Maybe they will hurt you, maybe they will help you, maybe they will have you wondering why. But ultimately, know they are setting you in a direction.

You are being guided.

And your guide is the wisest, most powerful companion you could ever know. Let go of all the small things that don't go your way.

Learn to have faith.

Let God go to work. You can't see the future. Only God can. So let Him lead you to your destination only He can take you to.

VERSE: Proverbs 16:9 "The heart of man plans his way, but the Lord establishes his steps."

unknown makers

Think back to this morning. Did you have an alarm set? Did your alarm go off? Did you without a doubt believe the alarm would wake you up? Who is it that created the phone or alarm clock for you and wired it so that you could use it without worrying whether it would work? You must have really had some trust in the unknown maker of such a small inanimate object to get you where you needed to be.

What did you eat today? Did you open up a candy bar or bag of chips? Did you drink out of a bottled water, pop, milk, etc.? Do you have any idea whose hands have touched those items? Do you have any idea who helped get that product into your hands? That must have required a lot of trust if you are choosing to put those things in your body and consume them without exactly knowing where they come from.

Why can't we have this kind of faith in God? Why can't we trust Him without any doubt? You've never met the maker of that pop or maker of the chips or maker of your phone, but you trust all of those things and have faith, don't you?

You may not be able to physically see God in the flesh, but He is always there. We need to do a better job of trusting Him to pave the way for our lives and get us where we need to go… without a doubt in our minds.

Learn to live with faith.

VERSE: 1 Peter 1:8-9 "Though you have not seen him, you love him; and even though you do not see him now, you believe in him and are filled with an inexpressible and glorious joy, for you are receiving the end result of your faith, the salvation of your souls."

allow God to show you

When I was in high school, I job shadowed someone at a college who told me, "Madison, no matter where you end up, whether you choose this college or another, you are going to be successful."

That has stuck with me a lot throughout the years as I have had to make a multitude of decisions since then.

Sometimes in life we don't always know what the "right" decision is for us. Sometimes we are stuck in the middle of an answer and it is hard to know what is best.

This is okay.

You cannot always control the outcomes of certain situations, but you can control your attitude. No matter the decision you make, you can trust in it wholeheartedly and fully. You can trust that God will show you the way if you trust and remain in faith with Him. If you let Him, God will reveal to you those successes He has planned.

Remember that life isn't so much about what happens to you, but how you respond to those things. It's your attitude.

A couple years later I can now say that that college is my home where I have truly been successful because of my faith in Christ.

It doesn't always come easy, but when you finally make a decision, don't regret. Because there is a reason you made the decision you did. There is a reason God gave you that heart in that moment.

Learn from it and move on. Keep a positive attitude.
Trust, and have faith.

VERSE: Jeremiah 29:11 "'For I know the plans I have for you,' declares the Lord, 'plans to prosper you and not to harm you, plans to give you hope and a future.'"

take the stairs

We try to take elevators when we need to take the stairs. You're wishing for the next best thing, you're worried about the things in your life, and you want to just keep going and get through. All you can think about is what the next floor will bring or what is yet to come.

Stop.
Slow down.
Take the stairs.
Quit trying to rush.
Take this moment in.

A few years from now you might be looking back and wishing you would've enjoyed the moment that's already past. The elevator is easy, fast, convenient, non-testing. Stairs require more work, they take longer, you might stumble, trip, and fall; sometimes you have to take them alone. The stairs are what help tone you – they keep you spiritually fit.

Embrace the time put into your hard work, the lessons you learned from all the stumbles, and take in the moments spent with the Big Man up"stairs."

VERSES: Jeremiah 2:25 "Slow down. Take a deep breath. What's the hurry? Why wear yourself out?"

Psalm 46:10 "Be still and know that I am God."

let it go

Worrying is a result of not trusting God to take care of us and our assorted situations we encounter in life. Worrying steals our peace, it opens up doors for the devil, and it wears us out.

God always has your best interest at heart.

How is worrying going to fix your problem or make it better?

It's not.

So, acknowledge it, pray about it, and let it go – God's got it in His hands. Trust God more than your feelings.

Let it go.

VERSE: Matthew 11:28 "Come to me, all of you who are tired from carrying heavy loads, and I will give you rest."

your heart

Learn to give God your heart, and He will place it in the hands of the one He believes is worthy of it.

Don't be caught up in finding the right partner, the right job, the right future. God will place the right things in your heart at the right time.

He has instilled passions within you. Don't ignore them.

He has instilled beauty, grace, peace, the right personality, the perfect laugh, strength, and love within you. Don't change that.

Trust. The only way we will succeed at being ourselves is when we have faith and trust in God; it is when we rid ourselves of all frantic pursuits and simply follow what God is putting in our hearts.

You will be guided to the right partner at the right time if you keep in faith with Christ.

You will be guided to the right career if you listen to what passions God has instilled in you.

You will be guided to the right future when you learn to simply let go of the control yourself and hand it over to God. Your dreams will come true when you pursue the desires God has given you to fulfill. There is a reason you have the passions and talents you do. God will help you fully live them out.

Listen to what God is putting in your heart. Don't venture off and worry about figuring it all out on your own. God is there all the time.

And when you feel those tugs on your heart, *act upon them*. No need to hesitate.

Listen to the Lord. Learn to give God your heart.

VERSE: Proverbs 23:26 "My son, give me your heart and let your eyes delight in my ways."

transforming faith

The Bible describes faith as substance. Substance is defined as, "the real physical matter of which a person or thing consists and which has a tangible, solid presence."

Faith is a real, true, life-filled thing. Although we do not physically see God or Heaven, we have a faith that allows us to believe in those things.

Faith is confidence. Faith is hope.

When we choose to have faith, our lives begin to change. We are less anxious, our attitudes become more understanding, we don't try to take everything on ourselves, and we begin to trust in God's plan rather than trying to write one ourselves.

Let me ask you this: do you trust and believe that Iceland exists? Have you physically stepped foot on Iceland or been there? I personally have not, but I have heard of people who have visited. I have seen pictures. I have learned about it in school. Although I have never been to Iceland, I still have faith that it exists.

God is like Iceland. We may not physically see Him all the time, but there is evidence everywhere that He exists. There are people that know Him, people who have felt His Presence, people who have seen Him working in their lives.

Have the faith to be one of those people.

VERSE: Hebrews 11:1 "Now faith is the substance of things hoped for, the evidence of things not seen."

communicating with God

Why should we always be in communication with God if He already knows what we want?

The same reason you talk to your mom or your dad or your best friend or your significant other.

Although those people may know you like the back of their hands, how would your relationship be if you decided not to communicate? They already know what you want usually, and they always decide to do what they want in the end, yet you choose to talk to them and communicate in order to have the best relationship.

This must be the same kind of thinking in our relationship with our best friend in Heaven.

Take the time to genuinely talk to Him each day.
He's an amazing listener.

And He always follows through.

VERSE: Matthew 7:7 "Ask, and it will be given to you; seek, and you will find; knock, and it will be opened to you."

our band aid

A band aid is defined as "an adhesive bandage with a gauze pad in the center, used to cover minor wounds." I don't know if it was just me, but when I was younger I thought band aids were the coolest thing. I would wear band aids on my head and stick them on my arms, my legs, my stomach... even when I had no injury. But still, I loved band aids. The only thing I liked about getting shots at the doctor when I was younger was the fact that I knew I'd get a cool band aid afterward.

I'd like to think of God as a band aid.

Some wounds are bigger than others – every band aid is a different size and shape. The wounds they cover are all temporary – they are minor injuries that will eventually heal with time. Sometimes the band aids fall off – they lose their adhesiveness and don't always stay on. This is usually due to our own doing – whether that is being active with other activities or ripping the band aid off once the wound has healed.

I'd like to think of this as our faith with God. Each one of us has our problems (our injuries) that we all have to deal with. God comforts us and heals these *temporary* wounds.

Whatever hurt we have does not last forever.

God is able to provide us with big aids and small aids, depending on our injuries. Oftentimes we are closest to God when we need something (a band aid for a wound), and when we don't feel the hurt as much we tend to get caught up in other activities, thus causing our band aids to fall off. We don't feel like we always need it. No matter what we are going through in life, God provides the healing.

He is forever our band aid.
Wear Him around proudly.

VERSE: Psalm 103:2-4 "Praise the Lord, my soul, and forget not all his benefits – who forgives all your sins and heals all your diseases, who redeems your life from the pit and crowns you with love and compassion."

scrubadub love

Choosing to have a relationship with God is like taking a shower. Showers are like faith.

Not everyone chooses to immerse themselves at the same time. Some people take long showers, others take short showers. Some are exposed to showers more often – they are equipped with the items necessary to cleanse themselves.

Some people jump in dirtier than others, some only choose to shower every so often. Some people are given the privilege to shower every day, yet don't share their shower items to someone who needs them. Some people sing in the showers; others do their best thinking in the shower.

Sometimes it's hard to get out of the shower; sometimes it's easy to get in the shower. Sometimes we're too tired, too sleepy, too busy, too lazy.

Through this all, however, we all go in dirty and come out clean. Having a relationship with God is so similar.

We stand as sinners, dirtied by our trespasses. We aren't always consistent with our faith – sometimes we make a commitment every day, and sometimes we skip a day.

Some of us have more weighing on our shoulders, some of us are more rundown by guilt, anger, frustration, jealousy (dirt). Some of us take a long time to talk to God and grow in our faith each day. Some of us only make a short time. Sometimes we find it hard to divulge into our faith, because we are often tired, sleepy, busy, or lazy. Some of us sing to worship God, others maybe meditate on the Word.

No matter what our lives look like, God is always there to cleanse and purify us. Immerse yourself in His love.

VERSE: 1 John 1:7 "But if we walk in the Light as He Himself is in the Light, we have fellowship with one another, and the blood of Jesus His Son cleanses us from all sin."

slow down

Too often in life we speed things up way too fast on our own.

We are planning for what we will wear tomorrow, for what we will do next weekend, for what we will do on vacation in a couple months.

We are always going, going, going.

We oftentimes forget to live in the present. We are so caught up in what's next or what's behind that we forget to seize the beauty in each moment. We forget to have faith.

Slow down.
Take a breath.

The only thing that is now is this moment. So soak it in, and fully live in the present.

Embrace this moment and have faith in whatever will be.

You do not know what tomorrow holds, and you cannot change the past. So take this moment, this minute, this second, and *live*. Without fear, without worry, without what-ifs.

Slow down, and take life one day at a time, one beautiful moment at a time.

Enjoy today.

VERSE: Matthew 6:33-34 "But seek first the kingdom of God and his righteousness, and all these things will be added to you. 'Therefore do not be anxious about tomorrow, for tomorrow will be anxious for itself. Sufficient for the day is its own trouble.'"

don't read into things

One thing people tend to do a lot of in life is overthink.

We let our minds wander a little too much, and we often come up with a variety of different situations that have no significance to what actually happens.

Some of this is from the fact that we want to be prepared – we want to brace ourselves for the worst in case it occurs. Some of this is out of insecurity – we sometimes feel people are against us when they really are not. Some of this comes out of jealousy – we tend to size ourselves up to others and analyze and critique when it is not necessary. Some of this is out of fear – we fear we are not enough.

Jesus did not intend for us to live like this.

Give your mind a break and relax. Life is too short to spend so much time on situations that don't exist.

Don't jump to conclusions.
You are more than enough.

Be happy and be light. Be still and have faith. Trust and love.
God is working and fighting for you every minute of every day.

VERSE: Exodus 14:14 "The Lord will fight for you; you need only to be still."

when things don't work out

There will be times in life where you think you have it all figured out.

You've got the right partner. You've got the right job. You've got the right preparation. You've got the right mindset.

But there will be times when things just don't work out.

Maybe your partner and you discovered your interests and priorities don't line up. Maybe you got let go from your job. Maybe your ingenious new idea got turned down. Maybe you've been really praying for something but it didn't happen.

Through all of this, life goes on.
Through all of this, God is right.

God can see things we cannot. He is all-knowing. Trust that He has your best interest at heart.

Look at it this way: Jesus did not want to go when he was on the cross. He saw the pain ahead and struggled with enduring it. But instead of rebelling or accusing or letting His emotions take over, He prayed until He had a change in attitude. What an example.

When God guides you down a path you don't want to go on, think of Jesus and trust that His ways are right. They are getting you to a better job, a better partner, a better idea, a better tomorrow.

Don't let your emotions take over in times of confusion or pain. Send it all up to God. Let Him take away your baggage and lighten your load with His guiding hand.

VERSE: Hebrews 13:5 "Be content with what you have, for He has said, "I will never leave you nor forsake you.""

our toilet

It's so easy in the world today to get caught up in running from one thing to the next. We are always distracted. We don't want to miss out on anything. Sometimes we become so busy in the world that we forget to be still. And sometimes we take on so much and begin to take matters into our own hands.

What a load.
When you think about it, God is like a toilet.

We have all this garbage we need to get rid of – this big load we need to dump.

Sometimes we get constipated and stuck in life – sometimes we aren't moving in our faith journey. Sometimes we eat or take in bad things that cause a bad load – this could be surrounding ourselves with unhealthy, negative people, placing ourselves in bad situations, etc. And it is these people and situations that can sometimes cause a clog. There is no movement and everything becomes stagnant. But, eventually, with some help, the clog can always become unclogged and God continues to take off your load. He lifts it off your shoulders. And he gets rid of it all.

So quit trying to take on everything yourself.
Take a seat and take a load off.

…I'm sorry if this grossed you out.

VERSE: Psalm 55:22 "Cast your burden upon the Lord and He will sustain you; He will never allow the righteous to be shaken."

faith without works

Faith without works is dead.

You can be the biggest talk of the town, you can be believing as all get out. But if you don't put your words into actions, if you don't stop talking and don't start walking, you will not get very far.

Understand that you can go to church, you can say you believe, you can proclaim many things. The important part is going to work.

It's getting your hands dirty and giving. It's following through with what you say. It is going out and acting upon what God calls for. It's not only believing in love, but showing love.

Follow your faith with action.
Go out into the world.
Be light.
Give.
Love.
Guide.
Protect.
Bind.
Nurture.
Act.

VERSE: James 2:26 "For as the body without the spirit is dead, so faith without works is dead also."

farming faith

Are you looking to grow in life?

I think some of us get into a slump and sometimes get stuck in a rut. We wonder how we can keep excelling. We say we believe in God and that we have a faith. We know God will care and provide for us and give us all that we need.

We have all these things.
But are we in an active frame of mind?
Are we making every effort to pursue God and our relationship with Him?

Faith is like farming.

You can be given all the land, all the tools, and all the seed, but if you don't put in the work, where will that get you? If there is no action what will you be growing in? If you do not utilize what you are given, what will you produce?

What Jesus calls us to do is act.
He calls us to farm.

Some will produce corn, some will produce beans, some will produce wheat. There will be good years; there will be bad years. But when our work aligns with what God has planned we produce the best crop.

VERSE: 2 Peter 1:5-7 "For this very reason, make every effort to add to your faith goodness; and to goodness, knowledge; and to knowledge, self-control; and to self-control, perseverance; and to perseverance, godliness; and to godliness, brotherly kindness; and to brotherly kindness, love."

pray with faith

Along with faith comes trust.

We must trust that God has our best interest at heart. We must trust that He is always working out what is best for us. We must pray without ceasing, always giving thanks, always being in communication, always letting go of our baggage, and always thinking of others.

And when you pray, you must have faith and trust that God is going to take care of you. He is listening to you. He is working within you. He is making sure you are set on the right path.

If you trust and have faith that God is working things out for your good, you will see these things unfold.

Don't be afraid to pray boldly. God is listening to every dream, every desire. There is a reason he placed these dreams and passions within you – He wants to help you reach them. Believe that.

God's got something perfect for you.
Have faith in what you're praying for. Know that God is there.

God's love for you is far too great for Him to let you miss your destiny. Trust in that.

You can pray all you want. You can ask for all you want. You can complain all you want. But unless you *believe* and *trust* and *have faith* that He is working all things out for your good, you won't get to fully experience the life He has planned for You. You must first have faith in His plans.

Pray with faith.

VERSE: Mark 11:22-24 "Have faith in God. Truly, I say to you, whoever says to this mountain, 'Be taken up and thrown into the sea,' and does not doubt in his heart, but believes that what he says will come to pass, it will be done for him. Therefore, I tell you, whatever you ask in prayer, believe that you have received it, and it will be yours."

something new

There will be some scary changes in life.

You might move somewhere new, you might begin a new relationship, you might start a new job, you might start raising a family, you might run into some challenges.

Change is bound to happen.

But through all of the goodbyes, the hellos, the old endings, and the new beginnings, you can trust and have faith that you're going to get through all of it. No matter how scary a change might seem to you, God will give you the strength and the guidance to get through it if you keep your eyes fixed on Him.

Think about Abraham.

God told Abraham to literally pack up and leave his country to start a new nation.

Can you imagine?!

God told Abraham that from him he would bless the earth. Although Abraham had a hard time understanding, he trusted God to lead him in the right direction.

That kind of faith is something to strive for. Sometimes God may call you to make a big change. Do not be frightened. God is going to fight for you, He is going to be there for you, He will comfort you, and He will strengthen you.

VERSE: Proverbs 3:5-6 "Trust in the Lord with all your heart, and do not lean on your own understanding. In all your ways acknowledge Him, and He will make your paths straight."

why do bad things happen?

Over and over again you will hear the question, "Why do bad things happen to good people?"

There are questions in life we just won't know until heaven's gates open up to us. But it is important to know that *God wants the best for you.*

It is evil that creates bad things. It is not God's doing.

As long as people choose to not accept God, evil will rule here. When people don't choose God, they allow the devil to enter their lives. They allow evil to live and rule around them.

God doesn't wish bad upon anyone. He wants to have a strong relationship with us; He wants to see us grow and strengthen every day. He wants nothing but goodness to live in our lives.

Trust in that.

Some things in life don't make sense. But don't take things out on God when it's not His fault. If your brother or sister made a bad decision on their own, would you lash out on your mom or dad because they are the ones who created them? No, your parents raised up your siblings, they gave them life, they gave them the proper tools to live, they gave them a lot of love, they gave them comfort and support. They have taught them to be independent. Unfortunately, that independence led to a bad decision. But your parents do not control your brother or sister's mind. It is not their fault.

Just like that, God has given us love, support, and independence. From this, humankind has gone down the path of evil. We have created it. God is trying to manifest good out of the evil produced.

Stop feeling anger towards God when He is trying to mend what we have broken.

VERSE: Romans 8:28 "And we know that God causes everything to work together for the good of those who love God and are called according to his purpose for them."

love

1 binding love
2 discoveries in differences
3 know yourself first
4 gratitude over attitude
5 love it all
6 what you need
7 pour out your love
8 embrace
9 love yourself
10 everybody makes mistakes
11 imagine
12 work on you
13 more than meets the eye
14 rid of anything but love
15 sweeter on the other side
16 like tomorrow is your last
17 greatness and fear
18 all ears
19 selfless over selfish
20 forsake the heartache
21 give 'em a chance

binding love

Love is such a powerful thing in life.

It binds.
It protects.
It abounds.
It radiates joy.
Love is the root of life.

It gives blessings when needed. It mends broken hearts when there seems to be no hope left. Love unites families, friends, groups, and countries.

Love is so important.

Loving others not only changes your attitude on life, it also changes your attitude and treatment towards others.

If we all chose to embrace all the uncertainties, all the doubts, all the fears and failures, and if we chose to learn and grow and love instead of mope and deflate and hate, how different would this world be?

VERSE: 1 Peter 4:8 "Above all, keep loving one another earnestly, since love covers a multitude of sins."

discoveries in differences

There are a lot of differences in life.

God often uses those very contrasting from us to help us learn something about ourselves we would've otherwise not known.

God will sometimes place difficult people in your life. But instead of trying to change them, let God use them to change you.

In life it is so important to learn how to deal with different kinds of people and accept and appreciate the ways they are different. Start having the determination to love and live with peace among everyone, no matter the different circumstances or personalities.

Accept people in love. Once we do this, we open up ourselves to learn something God is attempting to teach us.

VERSE: Galatians 3:28 "There is neither Jew nor Greek, there is neither slave nor free, there is no male and female, for you are all one in Christ Jesus."

know yourself first

Love is awesome. It's an amazing, amazing thing.

And when we have those feelings towards someone, it is easy to get lost in it. It is easy for your identity to become intermixed with theirs.

Know who you are in Christ first.

Know what you stand for, know what makes you cry, what makes you laugh, what makes you full of life.

Understand that you are your own person and you must love yourself and know yourself before you can be ready to love another person.

Don't let who you are become solely dependent on one person. Surround yourself with a multitude of people who bring joy and light into your life, who uplift you.

Make time for friends, and make time for family. Don't be so caught up in a relationship that you totally forget to care for the people around you too.

Love with all you have, but learn to have balance with yourself. A relationship should not cause you to lose yourself; it should help you to discover the great things you did not see before.

VERSE: Psalm 143:8 "Let the morning bring me word of your unfailing love, for I have put my trust in you. Show me the way I should go, for to you I entrust my life."

gratitude over attitude

In life it's so easy to get caught up in our own little messes that we forget about those around us. We become so fixated on what's next in our lives that we forget to love and care for others.

I am beyond guilty of this within my life. I often worry about what's next on the agenda and don't take the time to tell those special people in my life how much I appreciate and love them. I sometimes make assumptions and don't think to be more understanding of others.

Everyone has their own messes, everyone's got something going on, and there's no need to criticize anyone because of their circumstances.

Don't become so caught up in your own tangle of messes that you forget to take the time to understand someone else's.

VERSE: Romans 15:7 "Accept one another, then, just as Christ accepted you, in order to bring praise to God."

love it all

I challenge you to love every second.

Love every heartache, every ounce of pain, every lonesome day or
night you may feel. Embrace those moments and love them,
because life is a gift, and you're being pushed in the right direction.

Love the grumpy old man that lives next door.
Love the way the rain falls on a stormy day.
Love the way your brother or sister gives you a hard time.
Love the way your dad looks at your mom.

Love with everything you have.

At the end of your life I hope you are able to look God in the eyes
and honestly, whole-heartedly tell Him that you loved with every
part of your being.

VERSE: 1 John 4:19 "We love because He first loved us."

what you need

Love the Lord above all else.

My hope for you is that you are so busy loving Jesus, the people around you, and life itself that you have no time for regret, worry, fear, or drama. When you choose to reach out to others, God reaches out to You.

But God doesn't always give you the people and circumstances you want. He gives you what you need.

There are people He places to help you, to hurt you, to leave you, to love you, and to simply help mold you into the person you are meant to be.

VERSE: Ephesians 4:2 "Be completely humble and gentle; be patient, bearing with one another in love."

pour out your love

When you begin to want the best for others, your life becomes better.

It becomes full of love and full of happiness.

Instead of comparing what we have or don't have to what someone else does or doesn't, decide to be happy for others no matter the circumstance. Pour out your love and be a contributor to the light in someone's day.

Accept who you are and what you have. Don't wish it all away because you're stuck in someone else's life.

Serve as an encourager.
Be happy for people.
Cheer them on.
Be a supporter.
Love.

VERSE: 1 Corinthians 16:14 "Let all that you do be done in love."

embrace

There are a lot of differences in the world.

Different beliefs, different languages, different traditions, and different backgrounds.

Each person has their own unique individual experiences. Those very experiences are what help shape them into who they become. You're not going to agree with everyone. There will be times when people will tell you you're wrong. You'll run into situations where someone will want to argue because of your differences.

I'm telling you now: *embrace those differences.*

Don't let them scare you. Don't let them keep you from connecting with people and getting to understand them.

Don't let disagreements discourage you.

Understand that not everyone sees the world the way you do. It doesn't really matter if you've actually got everything figured out... someone won't agree with it.

You could be the best ice cream cone ever made, but there will be some who don't like ice cream (this is definitely not me just so we're clear).

Embrace differences, don't fret over disagreements, and learn to love and understand. Do not be discouraged. God is with you.

VERSE: Philippians 2:1-4 "So if there is any encouragement in Christ, any comfort from love, any participation in the Spirit, any affection and sympathy, complete my joy by being of the same mind, having the same love, being in full accord and of one mind. Do nothing from rivalry or conceit, but in humility count others more significant than yourselves. Let each of you look not only to his own interests, but also to the interests of others."

love yourself

Although it is important to love others, you must also know how to love yourself.

I am very guilty of being self-critical throughout my day. It is easy to find my flaws and downfalls. Sometimes I get so busy in admiring others that I forget all that I am.

Learn to love yourself.

God did not send his son to die for us so that we would hate ourselves or not accept or love who we are.

Love yourself.

Let your life transform into a more positive and confident one. Let your heart be filled with peace and joy; love every inch of you.

You are the only person you must deal with every second of every day, so learn to love what you have, learn to love what you don't have, and love yourself.

This very thing will change the way you live your life.

VERSE: Proverbs 19:8 "To acquire wisdom is to love oneself; people who cherish understanding will prosper."

everybody makes mistakes

Love and forgiveness go hand in hand.

It is hard to live a joyful, loving life when we still have anger or bitterness toward someone who did us wrong. It's really hard.

Sometimes people do stupid things. And sometimes those stupid things can really hurt you.

You have got to understand that holding grudges and choosing anger over love only hinders your time here.

Learn to let go.
Forgive.

How does this happen? Pray about it. Pray for your enemies. No matter how weird or uncomfortable it may seem, pray for them. Want the best for them despite any wrong done to you.

With love there's got to be some forgiveness. Learn to let go, and understand that people just make mistakes.

VERSE: Colossians 3:13 "Bear with each other and forgive one another if any of you has a grievance against someone. Forgive as the Lord forgave you."

imagine

Imagine if we all actually loved how we are supposed to.

Imagine if we all loved with patience, kindness, truthfulness, trust, and perseverance.

Imagine if we did not keep any record of wrongs.

Imagine if we did not get jealous at our partners or friends or family members.

Imagine if we took the time each day to truly *love*.

Imagine how much better the world would be.

VERSE: 1 Corinthians 13:4-8 "Love is patient, love is kind. It does not envy, it does not boast, it is not proud. It does not dishonor others, it is not self-seeking, it is not easily angered, it keeps no record of wrongs. Love does not delight in evil but rejoices with the truth. It always protects, always trusts, always hopes, always perseveres."

work on you

You must learn to love yourself before you love someone else.

It's hard to love someone else when you can't fully embrace who you are. By loving yourself you come to know yourself. You learn and you grow and you strengthen.

We're all just human here.

There's no need to compare. There's no need to get nervous around certain people. There's no need to question yourself because of the words or actions of others.

Embrace and love who you are. Grow in your faith, and build your relationship with God each day.

VERSE: 2 Timothy 1:7 "For the Spirit God gave us does not make us timid, but gives us power, love, and self-discipline."

more than meets the eye

It's really hard not to judge people based on a first impression.

It's sometimes really hard to look for strictly the good instead of the bad. Sometimes our frustration, our jealousy, our anger, or our own mindsets can get in the way of seeing who people truly are. We oftentimes build up walls and don't try to understand others.

Just recently I went on a service trip where I worked for an older lady who at first didn't give off the best impression as we were redoing the floors in her home. Many of us on the service trip were sort of frustrated at the fact that we had spent money to give back and this woman who we traveled miles and miles to serve didn't seem to be too grateful.

By our last day, the lady we were serving had tear-filled eyes and a quivering smile. She told us how she would never forget us and how much we changed her life. She told us how grateful she was and that God had sent us to her. It was clear to us then that all along she had been grateful… It had just been hard for her to envision what we were going to be doing. Thirteen strangers coming into her home and moving all of her stuff around probably wasn't the easiest thing to see. I made the mistake of judging her personally for it.

By the end of our time with her, I was able to see how great she was and how thankful she actually was.

Take the time to get to know people. There's so much more than meets the eye.

VERSE: 1 Peter 3:8 "Finally, all of you, have unity of mind, sympathy, brotherly love, a tender heart, and a humble mind."

rid of anything but love

In pretty much every aspect of our lives we can ask, "Am I doing this with love? Am I performing this act out of love?" If the answer is a recurring "yes" then I believe your life is probably pretty fulfilled.

If we got up each morning with love, if we greeted every person we encountered with love, if we let go of all the anger, bitterness, jealousy, and comparisons and chose love instead, this world would look brand new.

Think about love.
It starts with your thinking.
It starts with a choice.

You can make money. You can receive awards. You can have a big house, a fancy car, and nice clothes.

But all that truly matters in the end is how you loved.

VERSE: 1 Corinthians 13:1-2 "If I speak in the tongues of men or of angels, but do not have love, I am only a resounding gong or a clanging cymbal. If I have the gift of prophecy and can fathom all mysteries and all knowledge, and if I have a faith that can move mountains, but do not have love, I am nothing."

sweeter on the other side

There once was a woman by the name of Miss Julia who had a whole bag of fruit. She lived in a small village with much hustle and bustle, and the woman knew the village would be moving soon to a better location with more food and better land.

One day the village decided it was time to pick up and move along to search for better. All the villagers packed up their things and started on their way. The woman went to grab her bag of fruit when she noticed that all of it was missing. She immediately felt anger boiling inside her and wanted to know who had stolen her fruit. As she began to follow the other villagers, she noticed a small boy at the end of her block who was struggling to carry her bag of fruit. The woman immediately ran over and scolded the boy for stealing her fruit and began to take it all back.

The boy meekly looked up at her and said, "Miss Julia, I was only trying to lighten your load. We all are moving, and I wanted to help."

Sometimes we jump to conclusions so soon in life. We don't take time to see the good, we don't always strive to bring out the best in others, and we often feel sorry for ourselves when things don't go our way or we don't understand something.

God doesn't give us what we want all the time; He sometimes sets us on twisted, windy, and unexpected turns. Sometimes people get caught up in feeling sorry for themselves and accuse God of not having their best interest at heart. Oftentimes God is just trying to lighten our load. He wants to carry our fruit so that when we get where we're going it tastes even sweeter.

VERSE: Proverbs 25:8 "Don't jump to conclusions – there may be a perfectly good explanation for what you just saw."

like tomorrow is your last

You've probably heard the phrase "live like you'll die tomorrow." Well, the same holds true for the topic of loving others.

Oftentimes we focus on people's faults; we form these judgements toward people because maybe we feel intimidated or threatened. We don't always take time to look for the good.

But imagine that you knew someone was going to die tomorrow.

Doesn't that change how you would treat them? Doesn't that take away all the frustrations or jealousy you have towards them?

We wouldn't let our fear of their greatness hold us back from treating them with love. We wouldn't be intimidated by their capabilities to make a difference. We would want the best for them. We would want their last day to be their best day. And I'm sure we would shower them with the love they actually deserve.

Well guess what.

Your last day could be tomorrow. The person you have some bottled up anger toward could have their last day tomorrow.

Let go of all the things that hold you back from love. Let go of jealousy, let go of bitterness, let go of anger, and let go of comparisons. Learn to live and love like tomorrow is your last.

VERSE: Ephesians 3:16-19 "I pray that out of his glorious riches He may strengthen you with power through His Spirit in your inner being, so that Christ may dwell in your hearts through faith. And I pray that you, being rooted and established in love, may have power, together with all the Lord's holy people, to grasp how wide and long and high and deep is the love of Christ, and to know that His love that surpasses knowledge – that you may be filled to the measure of all the fullness of God."

greatness and fear

People are afraid of greatness.

Vincent van Gogh, who sold one painting in his lifetime, now has pieces of art valued at millions. Galileo Galilei, who was criticized and judged for his theories during his lifetime, is now known as one who played a major role in the scientific revolution. Edgar Allan Poe, who was never able to make enough money to sustain himself, is now well-known for the new writing style he introduced to the world.

There have been so many people who didn't become famous until after their death. They didn't get the recognition or approval while they were living, because people didn't give them a chance due to their threatening greatness.

People are afraid of excellence.

Think of all the more love those people would have received had they been given a chance while they were alive. Think about how much better their lives would have been.

Give people a chance.

Allow people to grow and excel.
Be an encourager.
See the potential.

VERSE: Proverbs 3:27 "Do not withhold good from those to whom it is due, when it is in your power to act."

all ears

One thing in life people often struggle with is active listening.

People don't take the time to hear out others and understand. People often make quick judgments and quick accusations to satisfy their discomfort or questions. We often become self-centered throughout our days.

I challenge you to become an active listener.

Take the time to truly understand what people are saying to you.

When others are talking, don't just be thinking about what you're going to say next. Soak in what is being said to you, and give people a chance. Open up your ears, and see where that will take you and where that will take others.

VERSE: James 1:19 "My dear brothers and sisters, take note of this: Everyone should be quick to listen, slow to speak, and slow to become angry."

selfless over selfish

Put other people first.

Get rid of self-centeredness.

Try not to get so caught up in your own life and your own busy schedule that you become consumed with only those things that pertain to you.

When we focus on ourselves, we miss out on seeing the needs of those around us. I challenge you to begin every day with showing love to others without expecting anything in return.

Give out a compliment to someone even if you don't know how they'll react, hold open the door for someone even if you are in a hurry, actively start hearing people out even when you've got a piled-high list of worries as well.

Start giving instead of taking. Start filling instead of removing. Bring light where there is darkness. Become aware of the world around you.

Let go of selfishness.

VERSE: Romans 15:1-3 "Now we who are strong have an obligation to bear the weaknesses of those without strength, and not to please ourselves. Each one of us must please his neighbor for his good, to build him up. For even the Messiah did not please Himself."

forsake the heartache

Heartache.

The breaking of you is the making of you.

Maybe they weren't the right person for you, maybe it isn't the right time, maybe God needs just you with Him at this time, maybe there is someone much better out there for you.

Maybe God took your Grandpa because you needed another angel to look out for you and your family.

Maybe you got a flat tire because you would have been in an accident otherwise.

Maybe your friend ditched you because it was a toxic relationship that needed to be stopped.

Healing and forgiving requires wanting the other person to be happy, whether it is with you or not.

Pray for them. Pray for the situation.

Unleash your frustrations and accept life. Give them to someone who will gladly take the weight off your back… Jesus.

VERSE: Psalm 34:18 "The Lord is close to the brokenhearted and saves those who are crushed in spirit."

give 'em a chance

Learn how to accept people. Don't be so quick to judge.

With every person you meet, make an effort to see and bring out the best in them. I am a firm believer that no matter the person, there is some good within.

Do your best to bring it out.

Don't be one of those people that others feel unsure around, that others feel hesitant with.

Be open, be genuine, and give people a chance.

You'd be surprised at how many amazing things can come out of one person just seeking out the best in another.

VERSE: Colossians 4:6 "Be gracious in your speech. The goal is to bring out the best in others in a conversation, not put them down, not cut them out."

beauty

1 you are enough
2 selflessness
3 make 'em shine
4 happy with who you are
5 greed
6 one of a kind
7 like ice cream
8 joy in the small things
9 love who you are
10 impress less
11 purpose, not paint
12 dandelions
13 don't worry, be happy
14 beauties to love
15 quality over quantity
16 take a breather
17 opinions
18 always do your best
19 not what the world wants
20 not a competition
21 breathtakingly radiant

you are enough

Today was one of those days where the devil consistently tried to tear me down. "Are you even really that beautiful? Are you really special? What do you have to offer that's different from everyone else?" Just worry and stress and insecurities that amounted to nothing. Why do we spend our time thinking and worrying about this stuff?

Sometimes we feel we have the expectations that we are to look, talk, and act in a certain way.

You do not need to meet these expectations.

The beauty of life isn't about rising above everyone else and being at the top. It isn't fitting into a mold so that you are accepted by the world. It's about bringing people up on your journey. It's about being yourself and fully living out the purpose God has for you.

Now that is beautiful.

You don't need to compare yourself and worry if you are good enough. You are more than enough.

You are breathtaking, and I hope that you can see it.

There is not another person like you on this planet. You are one of a kind. Be the best *you* can be. Embrace every aspect of who you are.

Don't be tempted by frets and worries and comparisons. True beauty is shining from the inside. It's being genuine, kind, thankful, loving, and resilient. Don't listen to what the world says is beautiful. You are enough.

VERSE: Galatians 2:20 "I have been crucified with Christ. It is no longer I who live, but Christ who lives in me. And the life I now live in the flesh I live by faith in the Son of God, who loved me and gave himself for me."

selflessness

My grandma has been taking care of my grandpa for years and years now. Not once have I ever heard her complain.

Through all the visits to the hospital and the stays with hospice, my grandma has stuck by his side without any complaints or hesitation. She pours out her heart, and genuinely and kindly loves him with all she has.

I went on a visit to go see him, and she sat by his side, held his hand with one hand, rubbed his back with another, looked up at me with tear-filled eyes, and said, "I keep listening to the song 'Always On My Mind' because he never leaves mine."

It took a lot for me to not burst into tears. Grandma loves him with the most selfless, genuine, and kind love. She wants him to be happy and healthy, and that's about all she's concerned with.

There is something so beautiful about that selflessness.

Sometimes I get so caught up in my own agenda and my own day to day tasks that I forget to take a look around me and understand what other people are all about. I think a lot of us get caught up so much into our own lives that we forget about those around us.

Be sincere.
Be kind and help others without expectations from them in return.
Go out of your way to do good works in someone's life.

Don't roll through the motions and get caught up in your own tangle of messes. There is something freeing about helping others out in theirs.

You will find a peace when you decide to liberate yourself of constant self-thinking. Look around you, and touch people's lives. You will find your footprints left on the paths of many.

VERSE: Philippians 2:4 "Let each of you look not only to his own interests, but also to the interests of others."

make 'em shine

People change when you change your attitude toward them. It's crazy what beauty you can see when you give people a chance.

Hate the sin, not the sinner.

Just because you don't agree with the actions of an individual does not mean you should form judgements based off those actions alone. There is so much more than meets the eye.

There are many times where I have misunderstood people and because of those misunderstandings, I have formed judgements. This has never led me to a good thing.

Understand that God has placed a special gift and talent in each individual. It is your duty to help others find their gift and develop it. It would literally shock you if you took the time to actually get to know people.

The attitude we have toward others could be a catapult for releasing their greatness.

VERSE: Matthew 7:1 "Judge not, that you be not judged."

happy with who you are

There was once an older gentleman who had been working at the same company for many years. He grew tired of the same hours, the travel, and the high demand that came with it. The job was everything he ever wanted when he began and now he had lost interest.

The man decided to quit.

He began to search for jobs and came across a job description in the newspaper weeks later. His eyes lit up when he read through the details of the job. The job would allow him to have secured hours, explore around the country, and utilize all his talents and passions.

With excitement and eagerness, he felt a fire ignite within him.

As he read further to get more information, he found out that the job posted was his old job. The company he had spent many years at was hiring for the position he decided to leave.

The man returned to work and told the company, "I was wrong. This is the place where I belong. This is what I've wanted all along."

It's really easy in life to grow tired of things. It's easy to take for granted the things we utilize or do every day. Just like the man, we become restless and sometimes ungrateful. We don't see all that we are, all that we have, all that we will do.

Be happy with who you are. Don't allow yourself to grow weary of accepting yourself. God has given you what you need. He has set you in the place where you belong. He has given you everything you are meant to have to make you the one and only wonderful you.

Don't become weary of who you are and what you have. Open your eyes. Look up. Enjoy what you have around you, and never lose sight of who you are in Christ.

VERSE: 1 Timothy 6:6-7 "But godliness with contentment is great gain. For we brought nothing into the world, and we can take nothing out of it."

greed

It's easy to want more once you have a little.

But God did not intend to provide for all of your greed. He intended to provide for your every need.

Don't let the "I want's" in life turn into the "I need's." God even said it himself: "life does not consist in an abundance of possessions."

It's not about what you have. It's about what you give.

Life is not about acquiring more money, more fame, more material things, more time, or more attention. It is not about desiring a bigger house, a better car, or a fatter bank account.

It is about inspiring others.
It is about admiring God's beauty.
It is about magnifying God's love.

You can't take anything with you when you go. The only thing that will remain is how you loved.

Now that is beautiful.

VERSES: Luke 12:15 "Then he said to them, 'Watch out! Be on your guard against all kinds of greed; life does not consist in an abundance of possessions.'"

Hebrews 13:5 "Keep your lives free from the love of money and be content with what you have, because God has said, 'Never will I leave you; never will I forsake you.'"

one of a kind

There are 7 billion people living on this earth. 7 billion. That's a whole lot of people. As I travel more and more, I sometimes find myself comparing, seeing how many people there are that are more talented, prettier, smarter, funnier, or wiser than I am. But I have also come to realize that there is not a single person on this earth who is me.

I am the only Madison Virginia Bloker there is on this entire planet.

And when I let myself be influenced and altered due to the thoughts, opinions, and actions of others, I jeopardize my uniqueness, and therefore, my excellence.

I am so much more than what this world may make it feel like I am. I am so much more than a picture on social media. I am so much more than a text or a snapchat or a call. I am God's child.

You are too.

I am one of a kind, just like you. And I will not let the world try to make me feel like I need to fit into certain standards or fit a proper mold.

There may be 7 billion people on this planet, but I will make sure that I am radiantly shining as my own individual, a genuinely beautiful soul.

Just like you.

VERSE: Isaiah 64:8 "Yet you, Lord, are our Father. We are the clay, you are the potter; we are all the work of your hand."

like ice cream

Beauty today is altered. It's twisted by social media, by magazines, the press. It's changed by Photoshop, coats of makeup, surgeries, and dollars upon dollars. It is defined by people whose job is to look pretty and glamorous. I don't know about you, but that is not the beauty I wish to attain. My beauty runs more deeply than that.

It is the smiles I give to strangers as they pass by. It is my understanding heart when listening to a troubled friend. It is the amount of work I put into everything I do. It is my tearful eyes when I'm proud of my sibling. It is my passion and desire to give back to something greater than myself.

Beauty is so much more than what society makes it seem today. It's not about notoriety, it's not about attention, it's not about money or glamor or pictures on social media. Beauty is about your heart, your soul. It comes from within.

And that, my friend, is what makes you shine.

Think of it this way: the beauty of a DQ blizzard from the outside seems nice, but the inside, with all of the ice cream inside the cup, is really what makes it beautiful. Can you tell I like ice cream yet?

VERSES: 1 Samuel 16:7 "But the Lord said to Samuel, 'Do not look on his appearance or on the height of his stature, because I have rejected him. For the Lord sees not as man sees: man looks on the outward appearance, but the Lord looks on the heart.'"

Proverbs 31:30 "Charm is deceitful, and beauty is vain, but a woman who fears the Lord is to be praised."

joy in the small things

Life is so beautiful.
And at times, it is hard to see all of the beauty.

There are struggles that come up, expectations to meet, money that needs to be made, meetings that need to be attended.

In the midst of all of this, it is so important to find joy in the small things.

Look at the clouds in the sky, the cute dog across the street, the old man holding his wife's hand, the birds chirping in the morning, the sun setting at night. There are so many small things to cherish and value, yet we look past the beauty in them.

Don't take them for granted.

When you feel life is getting too tense, when you can feel the pressure around you, when things begin to feel dull, take a step back and find joy in the small things.

They are, after all, the big things.

VERSE: John 15:11 "These things I have spoken to you, that my joy may be in you, and that your joy may be full."

love who you are

Think: What is something you have from the day you're born until the day you die? Nothing? Okay, what is something you have for an extended period of time throughout your life? Do you ever grow tired of that thing? New shoes? Nahh, that style went out two months ago. Nice new shirt? Nahh, there was a nicer one that fit a whole lot better today in the store.

The only thing you must constantly deal with every second of every day of your life is yourself. You must wake up, look in the mirror and see yourself. You must look in your closet and look down at your body to dress yourself. You must listen to yourself speak every day. You must deal with every thought that comes into your mind.

No wonder people find it so hard to love themselves!

In today's booming culture, it's all about finding the next best thing. It's all about going fast, having the nicest clothes, the coolest shoes, the nicest car. We go through items in our lives like I do ice cream.

An insane amount.

Start loving yourself and realize that the flaws you see are sometimes a result of over analyzing every inch of you. God crafted you. Don't insult his art.

You are *loved*. So greatly.

You were not created to be enough for the world. Heck, you weren't even created for this *world*. You were created to find radiance and joy in the purpose God has given you.

VERSE: 1 Corinthians 6:19-20 "Or do you not know that your body is a temple of the Holy Spirit within you, whom you have from God? You are not your own, for you were bought with a price. So glorify God in your body."

impress less

You know what is absolutely beautiful?
When people don't live to impress others.

When people are genuine and true, there is something about them that makes them shine a little more. It makes them brighter and they give off a very rare beauty. This life is not about performing for an audience. Life should not be lived by a constant conquest to get approval from others.

Life is about love and passion.

It's about finding what ignites that flame in your heart and fueling that flame into a fire.

God has so many wonderful things for you and has created you to be more beautiful than you know. Don't bend and alter your beauty to fit into a certain way of acceptance. Don't live for the audience.

Live for that passion.

VERSE: Ephesians 2:10 "For we are his workmanship, created in Christ Jesus for good works, which God prepared beforehand, that we should walk in them."

purpose, not paint

That girl got 100 likes in 9 minutes? That guy has over 10,000 followers? Who gives a flying fish.

This life is not about getting attention. This life is not about painting the best picture of your life for the world to see. This life is not about gaining followers and posing for pictures and investing so much time into edits and captions and filters to gain acceptance.

It's about fulfilling your purpose and bringing people up along the way.

Your most beautiful trait is your ability to walk with and have a relationship with God. You must know your worth. God will provide for you and what you truly need.

You are breathtakingly radiant.

VERSE: 1 Peter 3:3-4 "Your beauty should not come from outward adornment, such as elaborate hairstyles and the wearing of gold jewelry or fine clothes. Rather, it should be that of your inner self, the unfading beauty of a gentle and quiet spirit, which is of great worth in God's sight."

dandelions

When I was younger I'd always try to find objects in the clouds. I'd go pick dandelions, thinking they were the most beautiful flower. But as I got older, clouds became things that blocked the sun, and dandelions became weeds.

Beauty used to be more than just a surface... It ran deep.

Growing older, however, makes it hard to not think, love, and embrace like a child. Look at a simple sunset. There is some beauty no amount of makeup, product, money, fame, or editing can even compare to. It's time to embrace the little things and find joy in them.

Look for some objects in the clouds and pick a few dandelions today. Don't get so caught up in this world that you forget to fully LIVE and see how beautiful this life really is.

VERSE: Job 12:7-10 "But ask the animals, and they will teach you, or the birds in the sky, and they will tell you; or speak to the earth, and it will teach you, or let the fish in the sea inform you. Which of all these does not know that the hand of the Lord has done this? In his hand is the life of every creature and the breath of all mankind."

don't worry, be happy

Beauty stems so much from happiness. I could not tell you a person I know who has been happy and did not look beautiful in that moment of happiness.

Happiness produces smiles, laughs, meaningful and lasting memories. Happiness creates joy and love and goodness. Happiness creates peace. And happiness all stems from you.

Life is 10% what happens to you and 90% how you react to it. If you choose to be happy as a reaction of those cards you have been dealt, I can tell you your life will be a lot more fulfilling and beautiful.

You will be stunning.
Don't let the dark times define you.

Choose happiness.

VERSE: 1 Thessalonians 5:16-18 "Rejoice always, pray without ceasing, give thanks in all circumstances; for this is the will of God in Christ Jesus for you."

beauties to love

Everyone has their own troubles. Everybody's got something going on.

People can pretend to be perfect, people can pretend they've got everything figured out. People can point out other people's flaws to make themselves feel better. People can judge others because they're so insecure about their own messes that they want to take the attention off of themselves.

Where does pointing out the troubles of others get you?

Nowhere.

Rather, make it a point to see the beauty in others.

Aim to be more accepting and understanding. Understand that everyone is the way they are for a reason. Remember that everyone is beautiful. Don't judge someone just because they sin differently than you. Imagine how much better the world would be if you chose to see the beauty in each soul you encountered. Don't look at other people as competition.

Look at them as beauties to love.

VERSE: Romans 15:5-7 "Now may the God who gives perseverance and encouragement grant you to be of the same mind with one another according to Christ Jesus, so that with one accord you may with one voice glorify the God and Father of our Lord Jesus Christ. Therefore, accept one another, just as Christ also accepted us to the glory of God."

quality over quantity

I once listened to a 91-year-old WWII veteran speak and he said, "Our lives are not about collecting things. It's about serving each other." That has stuck with me.

It doesn't matter how much money you have. Life is about becoming rich in love, not dollars.

It doesn't matter how many clothes you have. Life isn't about obsessing over items and how you look.

It doesn't matter how many likes you get. It doesn't matter how many followers you have. It doesn't matter how many people comment on your things. Gaining all of these things don't make you a better person. Life isn't about approval.

It doesn't matter how much you say you do. It's about what you get out of what you do. It's about finding fulfillment and applicable lessons out of these things.

It doesn't matter how many people like you or how many people dislike you. You have God on your side – isn't that enough?

It doesn't matter if you live to be 96 or 10. You can live a short life or you can live a long life – it's all about how you spend your days.

Life is about the quality, not the quantity.

It's about what you give and how you love, not who you gain the approval of or how much you receive.

VERSE: Matthew 6:19-21"Do not lay up for yourselves treasures on earth, where moth and rust destroy and where thieves break in and steal, but lay up for yourselves treasures in heaven, where neither moth nor rust destroys and where thieves do not break in and steal. For where your treasure is, there your heart will be also."

take a breather

It is so wonderful how natural it is to recognize God's beauty.

Today I was staring at a long list of to-do's waiting to get done. As I began to feel overwhelmed, I asked God for peace and comfort. I knew that in order to achieve these things I would need to step away from the tasks at hand and just take a breath.

I hopped on a bike and started riding around. The sidewalk was closed where I normally go. As I was about to turn back, I noticed a young boy and his dad coming from another trail I had never been on. I decided to give the new trail a try.

And wow, was it beautiful.

It led me through timber and tall grass and a beautiful stream, ultimately bringing me to a perfect view of the sunset reflecting over the water, with its colors dazzling in the water's reflection. It was beautiful.

And from that moment I felt peace.

I wasn't even thinking about what had to get done. I was enjoying God's beauty.

Whenever you're feeling overwhelmed, ask God to give you His peace, step away from the situation, and take some time to admire God's handiwork. It's breathtaking.

VERSE: Isaiah 55:12 "You will go out in joy and be led forth in peace; the mountains and hills will burst into song before you, and all the trees of the field will clap their hands."

opinions

People will have differing views on things.

Some will make assumptions. Some people will jump to conclusions.
Sometimes people will love. Sometimes people will hate. Sometimes
people will see the buds. Sometimes people will see the thorns. Some
people will say you're ordinary. Some people will say you're extraordinary.
Some people will like you. Some people will dislike you.

If there are all these differing opinions, if all these people have different
views, why are you getting so caught up in trying to please everyone?

It's impossible.

There are simply some people in life who do not understand your journey.
These are the people that are not meant for *your* journey.

Do not waste so much energy on whether or not you are succeeding at
gaining acceptance from everyone. It's simply not going to happen. That's
not your job to do.

Your job is to stay in your lane and follow the path God is leading you on.
Keep your eyes fixed on Him, and do not waiver or get sidetracked by
things that only lead to wrong turns.

There will always be opinions. There will always be differing views. You
cannot control what other people say or what other people do or how
other people feel. But you can control how you live your life and who you
live it for.

You can remember that you are beautiful. Life is not a game of
acceptance and pleasing. It is an expression of your love for Jesus Christ.
It is fulfilling your purpose God has for you.

Let go of the pressure to please. Live your life happily, and the right
people will find you.

VERSE: Philippians 2:14-15 "Do everything without grumbling or
arguing, so that you may become blameless and pure, 'children of
God without fault in a warped and crooked generation.' Then you will
shine among them like stars in the sky as you hold firmly to the word
of life."

always do your best

Have you ever met someone who gives their best no matter the task?

They pour out everything they have and don't rest until they finish what they set out to do to the best of their ability. They battle through tough times, they overcome obstacles, and they stay uplifted with a positive attitude.

How beautiful is that.

No matter what you do in life, strive to always give your best. What you plant now will soon be harvested.

And this doesn't mean just doing your best when there's a crowd. This means doing your best when no one is looking.

This is how you shine.
This is how you radiate beauty.

Use every drop of talent God has given you, and understand that your best isn't meant to be sized up to someone else's.

Be the best *you* can be.

VERSE: 1 Corinthians 10:31 "So, whether you eat or drink, or whatever you do, do all to the glory of God."

not what the world wants

It's not about what the world says you should be.
It's not about what the world wants to see.
It's not about what the world accepts.
It's not about what the world portrays as beauty.
It's not about what the world says about fitting in.

You weren't made for the world.

Think about a snowflake.

Every single snowflake is totally unique. There are no two snowflakes that are the exact same. They are all beautiful in their own ways.

Do you look at two snowflakes and try to see which one is better? What is the basis of your judgment? Is there any purpose in trying to pick out the most beautiful one? Aren't they both uniquely wonderful and beautiful?

That is exactly how God made us.
That is exactly how God sees us.

God looks at the heart. When he thinks of drop-dead gorgeous, he is thinking of your soul.

It's not about the world's beauty.
It's not about what the world wants.

Pray, keep developing your relationship with God, serve, give back, and always keep your eyes fixed on Christ.

Aim to have a beautiful heart *for God*, not for the world.

VERSE: Romans 12:2 "Do not be conformed to this world, but be transformed by the renewal of your mind, that by testing you may discern what is the will of God, what is good and acceptable and perfect."

not a competition

In life you will have to deal with imperfections.

Somedays you'll have to look in that mirror and stare down that zit or you'll feel like you need to lose ten pounds. You'll see stretch marks. You'll see bags under your eyes. You'll have to deal with frizzy hair. You'll compare, you'll fuss, you'll feel insecure at times.

But there is something you should know:
Everyone has imperfections.

Despite what you think, no one is perfect. Everyone has to deal with faults and flaws.

God didn't create us to compete with each other. Just because there's another beautiful person in the room doesn't mean you need to size yourself up or compete with them.

You have been fearfully and wonderfully made. God did not make any mistakes. Realize that your imperfections make you who you are. They are the things that set you apart.

External beauty will fade. Wrinkles will appear. Things will get baggy; things will get saggy. But the most beautiful things you can practice now are love, kindness, compassion, and acceptance. That beauty is timeless and it doesn't fade as the days go by.

Life is not a competition.

The goal in life isn't to win and beat everybody. It is to learn, to grow, to love, to inspire, and to bring out the beauty in others, resulting in the unveiling of yours as well.

VERSE: 2 Corinthians 4:16 "So we do not lose heart. Though our outer self is wasting away, our inner self is being renewed day by day."

breathtakingly radiant

Every inch of you, He created. Every curl around your face you try to straighten every morning, every freckle you attempt to cover up with makeup. He created your body shape, your facial features, your beautiful hair you always complain of. You have been created in the image of Him. Despite what you or others may think, you are altogether lovely and beautiful. The world can and will say a lot of things – sometimes it'll make you think you aren't pretty or skinny or beautiful enough.

The world is wrong.

To be completely honest, you'll find more joy in this life if you choose to walk with Him rather than believing it's better when you look like some photo-shopped image of a broken girl trying to prove she isn't.

You are a work of art.

You have been shaped into who you are for a reason. The characteristics He has given you, the experiences He has presented to you, the people He has brought into your life – He continues to mold you into the beautiful individual you strive to be every day. Every inch of you is breathtaking, but the most beautiful trait is your ability to walk with and have a relationship with God.

Know your worth.

Your purpose in life is far greater than any accessory you could attain in the world.

You are breathtakingly radiant.

VERSE: Psalm 139:13-14 "For you created my inmost being; you knit me together in my mother's womb. I praise you because I am fearfully and wonderfully made; your works are wonderful, I know that full well."

70

confidence

1 apples and oranges
2 dare to be you
3 quit comparing
4 not entitled
5 only motivators
6 identity in Christ
7 only cater if you're a waiter
8 confidently captivating
9 goal control
10 take a leap
11 born to fly
12 remove the need to prove
13 let go and let God
14 be adventurous
15 you are capable
16 enjoy today
17 one life
18 be childish
19 life goes on
20 keep the cards you're dealt
21 more than enough

apples and oranges

What's better: a spoon or a fork?
What about a flip flop or a tennis shoe?
An apple or an orange?

Your answer probably lies somewhere within the realm of "well, it depends." And you would be absolutely right.

We use a spoon for some things and a fork for others. A fork wouldn't be able to pick up our soup effectively, and a spoon wouldn't be able to wind up our spaghetti easily.
A flip flop is great for the beach, but not great for a run.
Some people like apples. Some people like oranges. We don't use oranges to make apple pie, and we don't use apples to make orange juice.

We all have different experiences, we grow up different, we sound different, we look different, we talk different, we all have different gifts, we all have our own passions and interests.

So why in the heck do we try to compare ourselves to each other?

Someone may not understand your plan because your plan is not theirs. You may try and try again to be like another person, but the truth of the matter is that you're not. You have been given so many wonderful talents and gifts and passions, and you are the only you there is on this earth.

Don't compare yourself to someone else's abilities or strengths.
Stay in your lane.
Your plan is not someone else's plan.
Keep your eyes on your own prize.

Don't risk losing your uniqueness as a mighty orange just because you see a juicy apple. You were not made to please everybody; you were not made to try to be like another.

You are wonderful and special.

VERSE: Galatians 6:4-5 "Make a careful exploration of who you are and the work you have been given, and then sink yourself into that. Don't be impressed with yourself. Don't compare yourself with others. Each of you must take responsibility for doing the creative best you can with your own life."

dare to be you

Be confident in who you are as a person and the abilities God has instilled within you.

Don't ever underestimate the power you have to make a difference.

If you have a dream, go after it. Don't let life hold you back.

Explore.
Jump.
Learn.
Travel.
Speak.
Smile.
Laugh.

Life is too short. Don't wait to follow your dreams.

Waiting produces wondering and wondering produces what-ifs. Choose failure over what-ifs. You will find your worst failures can lead you to your greatest successes.

Even the best had to fail to get what they wanted.

VERSE: 1 Corinthians 15:58 "Therefore, my dear brothers and sisters, stand firm. Let nothing move you. Always give yourselves fully to the work of the Lord, because you know that your labor in the Lord is not in vain."

quit comparing

"The only person you should try to be better than is the person you were yesterday."

Being a competitor, I oftentimes find myself comparing. And it never makes me feel good.

I find myself wanting to beat out other people rather than making myself better. Trust me when I say that you will feel so much better if you work on improving yourself for *you* rather than for the satisfaction of being better than another.

God didn't create you to be exactly like someone else.

He gave you your strengths and talents and abilities for a reason. Focus on your own strengths, not on someone else's. Understand that you aren't going to be perfect. Understand that no one is.

Don't knock other people down because you feel insecure about their strengths compared to yours. Supporting others in their successes will ultimately lead you to more success as well.

You've got to realize that what you have is enough. And you've got to love what you have. If you're always seeking out to attain what others have, you will never have enough.

Know that you have more than enough.

VERSE: Galatians 1:10 "For am I now seeking the approval of man, or of God? Or am I trying to please man? If I were still trying to please man, I would not be a servant of Christ."

not entitled

Remember in life that you are not entitled. No matter your name, your successes, your money, your race, your talents, your wisdom, you are not always right.

Keep yourself in check.

There are times when you will feel great. There are times when you will feel down. There will be times when people will laugh at your jokes. There will be times when people stare at you blankly. There are times when people will agree with you. There will be times when people totally disagree with you.

Remain uplifted through all of it.

The truth of the matter is that life isn't always what you want. God doesn't always give you what you want. He places things in your life to help you grow, to help you excel, to help mold you into the right person. But remember that that person is always being molded.

There is always more to learn.
You do not know everything, and there are going to be some things you just don't understand.

Accept people. They may see the world differently than you. That doesn't make you better. That doesn't make them better. But train your mind to keep yourself in check and always look for the good.

Understand and accept.
Don't allow entitlement to loom over your dwelling.

VERSE: Ephesians 4:1-6 "As a prisoner for the Lord, then, I urge you to live a life worthy of the calling you have received. Be completely humble and gentle; be patient, bearing with one another in love. Make every effort to keep the unity of the Spirit through the bond of peace. There is one body and one Spirit, just as you were called to one hope when you were called; one Lord, one faith, one baptism; one God and Father of all, who is over all and through all and in all."

only motivators

There will be people in life who will make you feel like you are not good enough.
There will be times when people try to bring you down.
There will be times when people will say mean things behind your back, even when you did no wrong.

Understand that those people have their own problems. How bad it must be to be so unhappy that they feel the need to bring someone down so that they can feel lifted up.

You are so enough.
You are more than capable.
You can overcome whatever obstacles you have.

You have Jesus.

You are already soaring above. Don't worry too much about what others are saying. Let them talk. Soon enough, they'll find out how much more motivated you have become because of them. Thank them for the obstacles.

VERSE: Romans 12:14 "Bless those who persecute you; bless and do not curse them."

identity in Christ

I find myself way too often comparing myself to others. I just feel like it's an easy thing to do in today's society. But every time I begin to size myself up to another, I only feel empty.

I am not fulfilled in a sustainable way. I don't make myself feel better. I am basically looking for another's faults so mine don't seem as bad.

When I make the choice not to compare, my mind and heart are filled with the right things. I see the beauty in others rather than any imperfections.

I don't treat life as a competition.

I realize it is not about who I am but whose I am. It's not about me. It's about Him.

I embrace everything I am, every piece of my imperfect being, and own it confidently, for I am the only me there is. I will not allow myself to sacrifice my identity by getting lost in someone else's.

Embrace who you are in Christ, and love it.

Don't risk your uniqueness by worrying about how you compare to another. Work to better yourself, not to be better than others.

You are beautiful just the way you are.

VERSE: 2 Corinthians 10:12 "When they measure themselves with themselves and compare themselves with one another, they are without understanding and behave unwisely."

only cater if you're a waiter

Attempting to be a people pleaser oftentimes correlates with a lack of confidence. It's hard to be confident in who you are when you are constantly trying to cater to the needs of multiple people with a multitude of differences.

Trying to please everybody also complicates things. Sometimes you forget who you truly are. You aspire to be what people want, and you oftentimes lose yourself. When you seek after God and discover and pursue the will He has for your life, that is when you will find yourself.

Don't let the desire to please everyone else get in the way of you discovering what God's intentions are for you.

VERSE: Romans 8:5 "For those who live according to the flesh set their minds on the things of the flesh, but those who live according to the Spirit set their minds on the things of the Spirit."

confidently captivating

More and more I am discovering the strength behind confidence.

Confidence allows people to soar to such further heights. You need to understand that not a single soul on this planet is perfect. When you quit allowing yourself to feel vulnerable or inferior to others, you let go of a stress that allows you to feel a sense of freedom.

Confidence is captivating.

A confident person has a certain light to them.

Remember that you could be the best country singer in the world, but someone is not going to like country. You were not made for everyone. You are everything you should be.

You have been created in the image of God.

Have confidence in that, and carry that confidence with you wherever you go.

VERSE: Philippians 1:6 "And I am sure of this, that He who began a good work in you will bring it to completion at the day of Jesus Christ."

goal control

Having goals is a great thing.

It's good to strive for something and always be seeking to be better. I think the problem today with our goals is that we get the wrong idea of what they should be. We start seeking after other people's lifestyles and achievements.

"They are relationship goals."
"She is seriously goals."

We start comparing and desiring to have what isn't ours. God did not create us to be like everyone else and seek after what others have. When you look to be like others you are sacrificing your uniqueness, and therefore, your excellence.

Look to be better for *you*. Life isn't about impressing people.

VERSE: Ecclesiastes 4:4 "And I saw that all toil and all achievement spring from one person's envy of another. This too is meaningless, a chasing after the wind."

take a leap

I attended a conference recently in South Carolina. I boarded on a plane all by myself, took a leap of faith, and left the Midwest to attend a conference out on the east coast.

I knew no one.
An absolute leap of faith.

The conference was to help me in my endeavors as a service trip director next year in college, and a quote they stated is sticking with me, "Never doubt that a small group of thoughtful, committed citizens can change the world; indeed, it's the only thing that ever has."

You can absolutely be that change.

Find your passion, find people that will support you, and absolutely go after what you want.

"It only takes one match to ignite a haystack, or one remark to fire a mind."

Get fired up.
You can make a difference.
You can shine in the dark.
You can go after what you love.
And you can change the world. Get going.

VERSE: Romans 12:6-8 "In his grace, God has given us different gifts for doing certain things well. So if God has given you the ability to prophesy, speak out with as much faith as God has given you. If your gift is serving others, serve them well. If you are a teacher, teach well. If your gift is to encourage others, be encouraging. If it is giving, give generously. If God has given you leadership ability, take the responsibility seriously. And if you have a gift for showing kindness to others, do it gladly."

born to fly

Fear keeps us from a lot of things.
Sometimes fear can even keep us from being who we truly are.

Too many times in life people are too afraid to go for the gold, to
reach out to someone, to make the first move, to take a big jump.
What stops them may be the fear of failure; it may be the fear of
what other people will say or think. I really challenge you to ask:

Who cares?

Who honestly cares whether or not you will stumble or fall? At
least you won't live with the wonders of whether or not that leap
would've had a solid landing.

You were born to fly.

No matter what you accomplish, no matter what you fail at, *people
will talk*. Unfortunately, the world is filled with judgment and
jealousy, but that shouldn't keep you from reaching toward what
you want so badly in life.

Take a risk, make a big change, impact, reach out, advocate, do
what you love to do. Go for it. The right people will be there in the
end. Have faith in that.

Let go of the fear of falling. Even if you have to stumble a few
times, eventually you will fly.

VERSE: Proverbs 3: 26 "For the Lord will be your confidence and
will keep your foot from being caught."

remove the need to prove

Just live your own life and let people fall in love with you for it. Nothing to prove and no one to impress. The right people will find you.

You are what you love, not who loves you.

Don't let other people's attitudes dictate how you live your life and how you treat others.

Not everyone is going to like you. But God did not put you on this earth to impress others. God only intended that you love them.

You can be the most glamorous flower in the garden and someone will find a wrinkle in your petal. Don't let what they say keep you from blooming.

VERSE: Proverbs 29:25 "It is dangerous to be concerned with what others think of you, but if you trust the Lord, you are safe."

let go and let God

You've got to learn to let go.

People are going to hurt you in life. People are going to say things they don't mean. They're going to nag and fuss and call you things behind your back. People are going to have bad days. People are going to disappoint you and let you down; not all will keep their promises.

The secret to happiness isn't controlling what other people do or say to you. It's not about getting people to like and accept you.

It's about accepting life for what it is and letting go.

Not everyone is going to like you. Not everyone is going to agree with what you have to say.

Accept that now.

And let go of people's mistakes. Let go of wrongs people have done to you. Could you imagine the list of mistakes God would have to read off to us at the end of our lives if He kept one? Accept imperfections and mistakes and all the bad you may see in others or in life.

Let go, and let God.

VERSE: Isaiah 43:18-19 "Forget the former things; do not dwell on the past. See, I am doing a new thing! Now it springs up; do you not perceive it? I am making a way in the wilderness and streams in the wasteland."

be adventurous

I challenge you to do something out of the ordinary.

Find a way to serve.
Travel.
Volunteer.
Think outside the box.

Don't feel like you are trapped into finding a job, settling down, and getting by.

Take a leap of faith.
Be fearless.
Be confident.

Find a way you can give back, and go explore. You don't have to get approval from others. It doesn't have to be something people normally go through the motions doing. Don't let fear keep you from fully living.

Take some time and explore. Money isn't everything.

Quit having fear of what is to come, and start doing what you love in the present.

VERSE: Ecclesiastes 3:12 "I know that there is nothing better for people than to be happy and to do good while they live."

you are capable

Why live in fear when you can do the impossible? You are capable of anything with the strength God gives you. But only if you choose to accept it.

There is a reason God has placed the phrase "do not be afraid" in the Bible 365 times. It is a daily reminder from God to be fearless. He has given you this life to use everything you've got.

He has given you this life so that you can be bold, daring, and fearless.

You were created to overcome obstacles. You were created to achieve greatness. You were created to make a difference. You were created by God, who painted the stars in the heavens and created the beauty of the seas.

You are powerful beyond measure.

He has given you purpose.

Be fearless in the pursuit of what sets your soul on fire. Remember that being fearless doesn't mean being 100% unafraid. It is being terrified and jumping anyway.

Give this life everything you've got. At the end of your life I want you to look into God's eyes and tell Him how you have used every ounce of talent He has given you.

VERSE: Matthew 10:29-31 "And the very hairs on your head are all numbered. So don't be afraid; you are more valuable to God than a whole flock of sparrows."

enjoy today

Always remember to live every day to the fullest, because you never know what day could be your last.

Enjoy youth. Don't wish for all the days ahead – live in the moment. Because someday you're going to look back and wish you had it all back to the way it was.

Be content in every situation, and do not let unfortunate circumstances bring you down. They are only meant to build you up. God puts things and people in our lives for a reason.

Have confidence in the Lord and what He's doing for you. He'll give you peace and remove doubt or fear. Trust and believe that all His works are good. He has given you today.

Embrace it.

Enjoy it.

VERSE: Romans 15:13 "May the God of hope fill you with joy and peace as you trust in him, so that you may overflow with hope by the power of the Holy Spirit."

one life

You have this one life. How do you want to spend your days?

Worrying?
Meeting deadlines?
Running in circles?
Holding grudges?
Regretting?
Making up false scenarios in your head?
Assuming?
Chasing after people who aren't meant for you?
Questioning?
Feeling sorry for yourself?
Being afraid?

Life goes by in a blink of an eye. Don't waste it on things that only weigh you down. Each day should be treated as a gift. Each day should be lived how you'd want to live your last. God wants you to have a full, abundant life.

Embrace yourself, embrace the day. Embrace the peace and joy God offers. Own who you are in Christ, and love this life He's given you.

VERSE: Psalm 94:19 "When anxiety was great within me your consolation brought me joy."

be childish

There's a reason God told us to be like children. Kids are stinkin' smart.

Think about how kids have to learn to walk.

No matter how many times they fall, they get right back up and try again. It might take some extra help from someone, but eventually they achieve their goal.

Children are persistent.

They do not give up. They accept help when needed and don't focus on the obstacles.

We all should start thinking more like children. Just like children, we have to learn how to walk. God wants us to learn how to properly walk in our faith. Sometimes we may fall, but God is always there to catch us if we accept His help. We need to learn how to focus on the goal and journey, not the potential roadblocks that could keep us from getting there.

VERSE: 1 John 3:1 "See what great love the Father has lavished on us, that we should be called children of God! And that is what we are!"

life goes on

Life goes on.

I often find myself getting so stuck in the moment. I often over-analyze and think too much about all that needs to be done, all that I have done imperfectly, what could or should have been. But once I learned to embrace and love the fact that life goes on, my world became so much better.

Even if it seems like the world is crashing around you or you didn't get enough things crossed off your list, or you said the wrong thing to your boss or spouse, *life goes on.*

You live, and you learn.
You make mistakes, and you move on.
It will get better.
Life goes on.

VERSE: 2 Corinthians 4:17-18 "For our light and momentary troubles are achieving for us an eternal glory that far outweighs them all. So we fix our eyes not on what is seen, but on what is unseen, since what is seen is temporary, but what is unseen is eternal."

keep the cards you're dealt

"Smart girls like to hear they're pretty. Pretty girls like to hear they're smart."

Be content with who you are and what you have. You were dealt these cards for a reason. What you're wishing you had is what another person wants to give up. What you're wanting to give up another person is wishing they had.

Don't compare your life to others.
You have no idea what their journey is all about.

Set your mind on the things above. God will give you the grace and love and tools you need when you focus on Him.

VERSE: Colossians 3:2 "Set your minds on things above, not on earthly things."

more than enough

A lack of confidence stems from caring too much about what others think. You cannot please everybody. Take Jesus for example, the king of all kings, who risked his life for you and all beings.

He was spotless, but yet the world decided to hang Him on a cross.

You cannot please everybody.

Use the confidence He has instilled in you, and don't let that be hindered due to the voices of others. Don't allow the noise of others to drown out your own inner voice. Save some heartache and worry, and realize now that the happiest way to live is for God, not the world.

The world will always let you down. The world will be quick to criticize, although sometimes it'll make you feel good. Don't let others' thoughts and opinions consume you. Don't let what they say affect who you are. Realize that no matter who you are, no matter what perfection you strive for, the world will say you are never enough.

But also understand *you are more than enough.*

Realize that your HATERS are only Having Anger Towards Everyone Reaching Success. If people are trying to bring you down it means you are already above them.

People only rain on your parade because they're jealous of your sun and tired of their shade.

VERSE: Galatians 1:10 "For am I now seeking the approval of man, or of God? Or am I trying to please man? If I were still trying to please man, I would not be a servant of Christ."

perseverance

roadblocks or stepping stones

So many opportunities are coming your way. So many talents and abilities and strengths are instilled within you. Your purpose He has given you.

This purpose is not easy. Life is not always easy.

Will you make mistakes? Yes.
Will you fail? Yes.
Will you at times feel like giving up? Yes.

But anyone who has never made a mistake has never tried something new. Anyone who has not failed has not stepped outside of their comfort zone.

In life there will always be obstacles. But those obstacles are what make you stronger. Sometimes you have to hit your lowest low to truly discover something about yourself. Use the roadblocks you encounter as stepping stones to get to where you need to be.

VERSE: Romans 5:3-5 "More than that, we rejoice in our sufferings, knowing that suffering produces endurance, and endurance produces character, and character produces hope, and hope does not put us to shame, because God's love has been poured into our hearts through the Holy Spirit who has been given to us."

when you make mistakes

There will be times when you don't do the right things.

There will be times when you think the wrong things and say the wrong things. There will be times where you'll put down the wrong answer on a test when all along you really knew the right one. There will be times when you let a negative comment slip out – maybe about someone, maybe about a situation. There will be times when you let people down. There will be times when you try to help but end up making things worse. There will be times when you just simply make mistakes.

That is okay.

Don't put so much pressure on yourself to live a perfect life.

It's not going to happen.

Accept what is, let go of what was, and press on toward a better tomorrow.

Learn.

Life is all about learning and growing and bettering yourself every day. Don't beat yourself up so much.

Everyone makes mistakes.

God loves you no matter the mistake. No matter how big or small, no matter the extent, no matter the impact, God forgives. Reach out and pray to Him. Ask for forgiveness. *Let go.*

Embrace the imperfections, let go of the mistakes, learn, and be ready for a new day.

VERSE: 2 Corinthians 5:17 "Therefore, if anyone is in Christ, he is a new creation. The old has passed away; behold, the new has come."

starting small, rising tall

We all start small.

A big oak tree was once a small seed.
A big snowman was once a small snowflake.
Steve Jobs was once just a young man with an idea.
Martin Luther King Jr. was once a man with a passionate calling.

Everybody starts at the bottom and works their way up. Everyone
hits a low before they reach a high. Trust that although not
everything will make sense at the time, it will make sense later.

As Steve Jobs said, you can only connect the dots looking back, not
forward. Steve Jobs dropped out of college and was fired from his
own company, and although that seemed to not make sense at the
time, he said it was the best thing that could have happened to him.

"It was awful tasting medicine, but I guess the patient needed it."
He found what he loved to do and went after it.

Don't settle.

True satisfaction will come from doing what you love, and if you
haven't found that yet, don't stop looking. Be able to get up and
tell yourself that if it was your last day on earth, you would be
happy doing what you're doing.

"Remembering that I'll be dead soon is the most important tool
I've ever encountered to help me make the big choices in life.
Because almost everything – all external expectations, all pride, all
fear of embarrassment or failure – these things just fall away in the
face of death, leaving only what is truly important. There is no
reason not to follow your heart."

VERSE: James 1:2-4 "Count it all joy, my brothers, when you
meet trials of various kinds, for you know that the testing of your
faith produces steadfastness. And let steadfastness have its full
effect, that you may be perfect and complete, lacking in nothing."

96

always do good

Persevering does not always mean getting through tough times.

It also means striving to live a good, true life each day.

We are commanded to never grow tired of doing good as long as we live. This means finding joy in our purpose and in loving those around us.

When I think of what is "good" I think of the fruit of the Spirit: love, joy, peace, patience, kindness, goodness, faithfulness, gentleness, and self-control.

Think of these things as you go about your day. Allow them to be something you live by every single day of your life.

Choose to be the genuine, loving soul that God has created you to be. Seek after what is good. You will be rewarded.

Never give up. Even when things seem to not go your way or when you show love but don't receive it, be resilient. Keep doing good.

Don't grow tired.

God has been here since the beginning, and His love for you only grows. Allow yours to do the same. Think about what is good, set your mind on such things, and live out that goodness that dwells in your soul.

VERSE: Galatians 6:9 "Let us not become weary in doing good, for at the proper time we will reap a harvest if we do not give up."

diligence

One quote I always try to live by is, "When I stand before God at the end of my life, I would hope that I would not have a single bit of talent left, and I could say, 'I used everything you gave me.'"

This quote reminds me of the kind of diligence God wants to see in our lives every day in everything we do.

Diligence is working hard, having a positive attitude, giving maximum effort, being reliable and responsible, and having visions and goals to work toward every day.

God calls us to be diligent in any task we do. Whether that is being diligent in relationships, in school, in work, in faith, or in our own endeavors. We are to act as if God is right beside us as we go about our days. We are to give our all and not let any talent or gift or opportunity go to waste.

Have a vision. Set goals. Don't just go through the motions. Find purpose in everything you do. Heartily live.

If you don't like something, change it. If you can't change it, change your way of thinking about it. Don't be stuck in a negative, slothful mindset. Stay sharp. Be tenacious. Exemplify diligence.

Lean on God when you grow weary. Ask for strength. But also know that He is always providing for you – you are always readily equipped to be diligent. You must choose to be so.

When the time comes for you to stand before God, I hope that you will be able to say you gave everything – that you poured out your heart in all you did and diligently lived a life to the absolute fullest.

VERSE: Colossians 3:23 "Whatever you do, work heartily, as for the Lord and not for men."

storms

Storms.
Sometimes they're pretty scary.

There are all types of storms people have to deal with. There are snowstorms, thunderstorms, hurricanes, tornadoes, etc. There are also life storms. And the storms of life correlate well with those of other natural disasters.

Sometimes in life, we suffer damage. We get knocked down. Sometimes the world seems to crumble down around us. Sometimes there seems to be darkness.

But there is one thing that remains consistent with every storm: they all pass.

Life goes on, and the sun eventually comes out.

Sometimes storms unite people, and everyone pitches in to mend the pieces back together; sometimes storms change people's perspectives, and sometimes storms teach lessons.

And from those storms we are able to learn, move on, and see the light. We are able to see the rainbow.

Don't let a storm keep you in the darkness.
Let God show you the resulting light.

VERSE: John 8:12 "I am the light of the world. Whoever follows me will not walk in darkness, but will have the light of life."

emotional management

Remember that you cannot base every decision you make off of emotions. You have to have a persistent, active attitude.

Don't let your goals or dreams be jeopardized because of your over-analyzation and overthinking.

Start putting your thoughts into actions.

Don't let fear or sadness or hurt or guilt keep you from what you want. Keep moving forward, even on the hardest days.

Right when you choose to overanalyze instead of do, you may become stagnant, waiting at a standstill. Don't be that person!!!

Keep setting goals, keep making action plans to see them through to completion, keep striving for them. Maintain the right attitude, and never stop moving forward.

Let God give you the peace you need to attain what you are seeking after. He will never fail you.

VERSE: Philippians 4:6-7 "Do not be anxious about anything, but in every situation, by prayer and petition, with thanksgiving, present your requests to God. And the peace of God, which transcends all understanding, will guard your hearts and your minds in Christ Jesus."

persistence in patience

Patience, patience, patience.

If God gave you everything you wanted when you wanted it what would you learn about your purpose?

It's not about getting what you want. It's about enjoying the ride of fulfilling that purpose. The setbacks you see now will one day be looked back upon as giant leaps forward.

It may not make sense now.

These tests of your faith, your C on that paper, the one who broke your heart, your friends who ditched you… they are getting you somewhere. They are getting you to where you belong.

Remain calm.
All is within reach.

Wake up with resilience every day, stay true to seeking out the path God will lead you down, and surely you will accomplish everything you have dreamed and more. Never give up. Successful people are not those who never fail. They are those who never quit.

VERSE: Hebrews 12:1-2 "Therefore, since we are surrounded by such a great cloud of witnesses, let us throw off everything that hinders and the sin that so easily entangles. And let us run with perseverance the race marked out for us, fixing our eyes on Jesus, the pioneer and perfector of faith. For the joy set before him he endured the cross, scorning its shame, and sat down at the right hand of the throne of God."

stepping back

I can recall one day at college when I had a piled-high list of things to do. Tests to study for, homework to complete, a room to clean, meetings on the agenda, etc. I was beginning to feel overwhelmed and kind of emotional.

I knew it was going to be a tight crunch for me to complete everything I wanted to. But instead, for my own wellbeing, I took a step back and took a deep breath. I enjoyed the beautiful night, I prayed, I smiled, I dreamed, I admired, I embraced the beauty. And by the end of it, I didn't seem so overwhelmed.

Although the to-do list was still waiting to be completed, it didn't seem so massive.

I was reminded of this today as my aunt came to take her kids to the waterpark for a family day.

She said, "It is so, so busy at work, but the kids didn't want to miss this. On the way here, I made a quick stop and talked to one of my clients who said that his 87-year-old mother's advice to him before she passed away was 'Make sure you don't regret what you didn't do.' He said, 'So take this free day even though it's a busy day in the office.'"

It is OK to step away and take a deep breath.
It is OK to look away from the pile of demands.
It is OK to start looking more toward what makes you happy and fulfills you.

Take a break once in a while. Relax.
Don't be so serious. Enjoy. Live.

Even God our creator rested after His work. Follow His example.

VERSE: Genesis 2:2-3 "By the seventh day God had finished the work he had been doing; so on the seventh day he rested from all his work. Then God blessed the seventh day and made it holy, because on it he rested from all the work of creating that he had done."

accept failure

Persistence is defined as a continued effort to do or achieve something despite difficulties, failure, or opposition.

Life is all about persistency.

Accept that failure is something that is going to happen to you in life.

There will be times of trial, there will be bumps in the road, and there will be obstacles to keep you from moving forward. Don't let small setbacks keep you from pursuing what you want or living out your purpose.

You are only as strong as you allow yourself to be.

As Nelson Mandela said, "It always seems impossible until it's done." Or perhaps Thomas Edison: "Many of life's failures are people who did not realize how close they were to success when they gave up."

VERSE: 2 Corinthians 12:9-10 "But he said to me, 'My grace is sufficient for you, for my power is made perfect in weakness.' Therefore, I will boast all the more gladly of my weaknesses, so that the power of Christ may rest upon me. For the sake of Christ, then, I am content with weaknesses, insults, hardships, persecutions, and calamities. For when I am weak, then I am strong."

like riding a bike

When riding a bike, there are a multitude of paths that can be taken. If given the choice, would you choose a path that is level and consistent? Or would you rather have hills, bumps, challenges, easy parts, and difficult parts?

Everyone is different. And no matter their choices, no matter their preferences, they all get where they're going. There isn't a journey God has set into motion that is better than another.

No matter the way and no matter the journey, God always provides the bike.

No matter the ups and downs, no matter the consistencies or inconsistencies, God is always going to pull you through. He's always going to get you where you want to go.

He'll give you the direction and guidance to take off the training wheels and travel down the path He has laid for you.

VERSE: Psalm 37:23-24 "The Lord makes firm the steps of the one who delights in him; though he may stumble, he will not fall, for the Lord upholds him with his hand."

resilient

Go ahead and raise your right hand as high as you can.
Go on – do it.

Now raise that right hand just a little bit higher.

Could you do it?

I once listened to a three-time world champion wrestler. Upon speaking to the big crowd of us, the first thing he told us to do was raise our right arm as high as we could. Hundreds of hands went in the air as people reached high towards the ceiling. He then asked us to reach just a little bit higher. I will tell you that every single hand in that stadium raised up just a little bit higher. He had so easily gotten every single person there to give 110%, more than they originally thought they could.

That is going above and beyond what you thought was possible.

You got this. Keep fighting.

Put your head down, and go to work. You've got plenty of fight left in you. You are strong, and you have so much to give.

Resiliency.

Wake up with it each day, and stay true to seeking out the path God will lead you down.

And when you don't think you have anything left, push just a little bit more.

VERSE: Romans 8:37 "No, in all these things we are more than conquerors through Him who loved us."

one step at a time

When you are seeking to accomplish a goal you have set out to do, it's okay to envision what exactly it is you want. However, don't get so caught up in the end result that you don't fully embrace every step along the way.

Sometimes in life we focus too much on the big picture and then as a result become overwhelmed. I find this to be especially relevant in running. When I go on runs and focus on my ending destination, I see the long distance I have left and begin to doubt and become discouraged.

On the other hand, I find that if I focus on one step at a time, each small destination is a victory and I am motivated by each one. Focusing on each small step makes it easier to get where I'm going.

Life is going to throw you curveballs. Don't be so caught up in trying to figure everything out and arriving at a certain point. God has a path for you, and He will set you in the right direction when you trust in Him. He will mold you along the way and help you discover things you would not have known had you tried to walk it alone. For every step you take there is another footstep beside you.

No matter the step, He will be there.

VERSE: Proverbs 19:21 "Many are the plans in a person's heart, but it is the Lord's purpose that prevails."

fear and worry

When we begin to excel or advance in life, the devil really tries to knock us down.

We see that we have good days. We see that we have bad days. There are days we are inspiring, and there are days we need to be inspired.

The devil attacks you whenever he gets the chance. Right when you begin to have a little doubt or have one of those bad days, he will jump on board to turn it into fear and worry. He will try to make you second guess and question your future and your impact.

Understand that you are capable of moving mountains.
Understand that you are capable of making a difference.
Understand that you are capable of overcoming all obstacles.

Do not let the devil trick you into believing you aren't enough or that you won't do great things.

When the devil tries to bring you down, know that greatness is in store for you. Know that you are close to leaving an uplifting mark that the devil does not want to see happen. Don't let him fill you with troubles or negative thoughts.

You don't need to fear or worry about what is to come. The future isn't even here yet. It doesn't exist. So quit worrying about the outcome or the results in the long run when all you can control is the now.

Know that you are destined for greatness when you keep your eyes fixed on God.

There is no need to fear or look so far ahead that you forget to give all you have in the present. Be consumed with God, not worry. Be consumed with uplifting thoughts, not ones that drag you down.

Move those mountains.
Make that difference.
Overcome obstacles.
You are more than capable in Christ.

VERSE: Proverbs 31:25 "She is clothed with strength and dignity, and she laughs without fear of the future."

until the final buzzer

Sports teach us a lot about life and a lot about faith.

If you're a good athlete, you give everything you have every minute you're on the floor or on the field. You strive to be better every practice and every game.

In sports you'll have victories. You'll have losses.
You'll have big wins and big upsets.
You'll have good seasons. You'll have bad seasons.
You'll have teammates.
You'll have teammates that let you down. You'll have teammates that lift you up.
You'll have people cheering you on. You'll have people cheering against you.
You'll have interceptions.
You'll have steals.
You'll have blocks.
You'll take hits.
You'll make mistakes. You'll learn from them.
You'll be behind. You'll be ahead.
You'll feel pressure.
You'll have to practice.

Now apply that to life.

Every day wake up wanting to be better. Practice good habits. Lean on your team. Learn from your team. Learn from mistakes. Accept differences. Take the hits. Become stronger. Learn how to handle the pressure. Celebrate the victories. Work through the losses.

VERSE: Philippians 3:13-14 "But one thing I do: Forgetting what is behind and straining toward what is ahead, I press on toward the goal to win the prize for which God has called me heavenward in Christ Jesus."

when people try to bring you down

You have to be odd to be number one.
And when you stand out and begin to be different, people won't always be so accepting. Bitterness, anger, jealousy, and regret can cause people to do and say things they don't mean.

And when people say or do these things, it's easy to get frustrated, angry, or upset. It's easy to wonder why they are choosing to be that way or wonder what you did wrong to make them say those things.

Understand that it's not your fault.

When people see you are excelling or rising to the top, a lot of factors can come into play to formulate their response. Some people become jealous. Others are stuck in their own failures. Some have low self-esteem. And others may just make bad decisions.

Understand that you cannot control others.

The first thing you should do if people are trying to bring you down is pray for them. Even if you don't think this will benefit you or matter that much, I promise you it makes all the difference in the world. When you choose to pray, you are letting go of emotional burdens including anger, frustration, confusion, and sadness.

And when you pray for others, pray for yourself as well. Pray to be more understanding and patient. Praying can open your eyes to things you did not see before.

As hard as it is, you must forgive. You must let go of what was said or done, and leave it in the past. Forgive. You will find yourself freed from a lot of unnecessary baggage.

Remember who you are in Christ, and know your worth. Remember that a tiger does not lose sleep over the opinion of sheep.

VERSE: Colossians 3:12 – 14 "Put on then, as God's chosen ones, holy and beloved, compassionate hearts, kindness, humility, meekness, and patience, bearing with one another and, if one has a complaint against another, forgiving each other; as the Lord has forgiven you, so you also must forgive. And above all these put on love, which binds everything together in perfect harmony."

109

living out your dream

God has instilled passions within you.

You know what they are. They inspire you, they excite you, they ignite that flame in your heart, they energize you, they make you happy.

You have dreams.

There is a reason you have these dreams – God has placed them within you.

But when we sit around and wait for the right time to pursue these dreams, they seem to never come and things never get done.

START GOING.

It is time to put those dreams into motion.

God has equipped you with what you need. God will provide for you in your pursuit of the dream. God will guide and set you in the right direction on your dream quest.

GO AFTER IT.

Don't sit around and wait for something to drop in your lap. Get moving. Start living out your dream. Pray to God, and trust in God. Put Him first always.

Find delight in Him. He will give you the desires of your heart.

VERSE: Ecclesiastes 11:4 "If you wait for perfect conditions, you will never get anything done."

practice patience

There is one quality that is so, so important that sometimes people forget to practice.

Patience.

Especially now when things are only a click or tap away, it is easy to want things right then and there. It is easy to become frustrated when the things wanted aren't received right away.

Learn to be patient.

Patience is not about how long you can wait. Many people can wait for a long period of time. It's about maintaining a positive attitude while waiting.

Understand that life is not a walk in the park always. There will be times that test you more than others, there will be hard, confusing times, and there will be times of waiting and waiting.

Trust that the timing is perfect.

God is ready at all times. He'll give you what you need when you need it and will take away when it must be taken.

Keep your trust in God, pray for patience, and all the right things will make their way to you at the right time.

Patience. Practice it.

VERSE: Romans 8:25 "But if we hope for what we do not yet have, we wait for it patiently."

astound yourself

I went to my little sister's track meet today, and I was amazed by how much speed and strength the runners could muster when another runner was coming up close behind them. Right when it seemed like they couldn't go any faster or push any harder, they found a burst of energy from deep within that was surfaced because of the competition they were up against.

The mind and body are so much stronger than we think.

If we really and truly push ourselves, if we give everything we have down to our inmost being, we would be astounded at what God will help us accomplish.

We all can do so many things we never thought we'd be capable of. Shoot high and shoot far, and when it seems like you can't go further, try to give just one more little push.

You will be amazed with where that can take you.

VERSE: 1 Corinthians 9:24-25 "Do you not know that in a race all the runners run, but only one gets the prize? Run in such a way as to get the prize. Everyone who competes in the games goes into strict training. They do it to get a crown that will not last, but we do it to get a crown that will last forever."

conflict

Conflict can be scary.

It's sometimes hard to know how to deal with differences or disagreements. God created everyone so uniquely and vastly wonderful that there are no two people exactly the same. With this comes various traits, lifestyles, expectations, habits, and passions. It is important to know how to handle and work through conflict when it arises, although there are situations that are never easy.

If there is one thing to remember it is this: it doesn't matter the number of differences. It's about how you *handle* those differences or disagreements. It all comes back to attitude. But when you are confronted with some sort of conflict remember these things:

Don't worry about the little things. Let go of what doesn't matter.

Understand and accept. Step into the other person's shoes and try to be empathetic towards their thoughts and beliefs. Hear them out. Open up your ears, and be willing to expose yourself to their ideas.

Communicate your expectations. Everyone has different ways of doing things, and everyone expects different things. Not communicating these expectations can lead to assumptions which typically are false.

Be patient. Think about things before you say them. Don't let something slip that you don't want out. Be patient with yourself and with others.

Let things go. Once everyone has shared what they needed to and have communicated what they wish, leave it in the past. Love isn't about keeping a record of wrongs or easily getting angered. It's about forgiveness, understanding, kindness, patience, and a lot of perseverance.

Look at conflict as an opportunity to grow. Look at differences as wonderful, wonderful things that keep this world colorful and vibrant.

VERSE: Romans 12:17-21 "Do not repay anyone evil for evil. Be careful to do what is right in the eyes of everyone. If it is possible, as far as it depends on you, live at peace with everyone… Do not be overcome by evil, but overcome evil with good."

full armor of God

The devil will do anything he can to tear us down.

It's easy to fall into the trap of his lies, guilt, and temptation. But you must call out and know what he is doing. You must keep your eyes fixed on God. You must choose to see light.

But how do we withstand all the evil in the world? How do we keep all the darkness from casting shadows on our light?

We put on the full armor of God.

In the Bible, Paul tells us all the things we must have to be equipped for this battle. We must first put on the *belt*, which secures the rest of our armor. The belt is truth. We should know God's truth and be totally truthful ourselves. Next we must put on our *breastplate of righteousness*. This means obeying God and living in love. This means asking for forgiveness and choosing to do what's right. We must cover our feet with the *preparation of the gospel of peace*. This means we must be readily available to speak the good news of God's Kingdom. In turn, we spread God's peace and love. Next we must wear our *shield of faith*. Faith means both believing that God is real *and* that He is working all things out for our good. When we have strong faith, we can withstand even the mightiest of blows. We will cover our heads with the *helmet of salvation*. Jesus has saved us. And from this, we can feel incredible peace and comfort. We must take with us the *sword of the spirit*, which is the Word of God. Remember that our sword will become dull if we try to figure it out all on our own. The Word can help us overcome anything. And lastly, we must *pray*. Pray unceasingly. This will help us keep the right focus.

Put on the full armor of God and withstand any discouragement, guilt, jealousy, anger, doubt, disappointment, pride, or any other battle. And always remember that you are never fighting any battle alone.

VERSE: Ephesians 6:13-17 "Therefore, put on the full armor of God, so that when the day of evil comes, you may be able to stand your ground, and after you have done everything, to stand. Stand firm then, with the belt of truth buckled around your waist, with the breastplate of righteousness in place, and with your feet fitted with the readiness that comes from the gospel of peace. In addition to all this, take up the shield of faith, with which you can extinguish all the flaming arrows of the evil one. Take the helmet of salvation and the sword of the Spirit, which is the word of God."

positivity

1 slow to anger
2 goodbye gossip
3 embrace the journey
4 don't be an "ass"umer
5 see the light
6 abounding surrounding
7 strengthened by setbacks
8 justin bieber and the present
9 watch the 'tude
10 it's gon' get better
11 speeding tickets
12 smile and shine
13 mindful of the mind
14 be the sunshine
15 meant to be content
16 self-made problems
17 steady and stable
18 dam right
19 train the brain
20 watch your words
21 every day is yours

slow to anger

The Bible talks a lot about being slow to anger.

I feel like this isn't something I pay a lot of attention to. When my little brother is being annoying, I feel myself getting mad at him. When I hear someone has said something bad about me, I feel flustered and tensed towards them. When things don't go my way, sometimes I get too easily frustrated. When my food isn't delivered on time, I begin to get hangry.

Wouldn't things be so much better if we would just relax? Wouldn't life be so much more enjoyable if we let things go and released our anger or bitterness towards those things?

Relax.

Life isn't meant to be a big frustrating task. Life is meant to be a beautiful gift. Don't ruin the gift by misreading the contents.

When things don't seem to be going your way, when someone doesn't say what you want them to, when your plans don't go according to schedule, *be understanding.* Understand that your little brother may be just wanting some of your attention. Understand that what you heard someone said about you isn't actually what they said. Understand that things aren't always going to go the way you want them to. Understand that your food tastes better the longer you wait.

There is a reason things are the way they are in your life. Don't be so quick to be bitter. Be gracious. Live in peace. Be understanding.

Let go.

VERSES: James 1:19 "This you know, my beloved brethren, but everyone must be quick to hear, slow to speak, and slow to anger."

Ephesians 4:31-32 "Get rid of all bitterness, rage and anger, brawling and slander, along with every form of malice."

goodbye gossip

Gossip.

Such an easy thing to fall into.
People talk, people seek acceptance, people fall into jealousy.

Do everything you can to not be one of those people.
Understand when something isn't your business.

Too often in life we try to fix problems that aren't even our own.
Let people live their own lives. Let go of the desire to fit in. People
who seek acceptance through attempting to fit in with everyone
else never get that far. They are too stuck in the need to please
people that they never stand up for what they believe because they
are afraid of rejection.

Accept right now that no matter what you do, someone is not
going to like you. Be who you are and speak up for what you know
is right, because this life isn't about pleasing the world.

Don't get so caught up in jealousy.
Jealousy can cause people to say and do some pretty crazy things.

Learn to love.
Learn to be happy for others.
Learn to be genuine and true.

When someone starts talking bad about another, you can walk
away, you can change the subject, you can stand up for the one
being talked badly about. But don't fall into the trap of gossip.

Let love triumph over the temptation to fit in or put others down.

What would you want others to say about you?

VERSE: Psalm 19:14 "May these words of my mouth and this
meditation of my heart be pleasing in your sight, Lord, my
Rock and my Redeemer."

embrace the journey

Have you ever taken an awesome road trip? Where you've hopped in a vehicle with others and just hit the road, adventuring out?

If you haven't already, I highly suggest taking one. It is after that experience that you will appreciate the winds and twists of a journey. You will appreciate how you got to your destination. And as you look back on your trip, you smile at the road that got you there and all the memories you made along the way.

I think of life in this way as well.

We often have our eyes on a final destination, a sort of end goal where we feel we will be satisfied if we reach it.

Appreciate the journey.

The journey and crazy ride, with all its twists and turns, are what make reaching that final destination extra special.

Understand that life doesn't always go according to plan.

Sometimes you run out of gas, sometimes you hit a bump in the road, sometimes you read the map wrong or the GPS says to turn left when you're supposed to turn right, sometimes you end up at a sketchy gas station. But take in these moments, and soak in all the lessons and memories.

Embrace the journey God has for you.
Embrace this journey we call life.

VERSE: Judges 18:5-6 "Then they asked, 'Ask God whether or not our journey will be successful.' 'Go in peace,' the priest replied. 'For the Lord is watching over your journey.'"

don't be an "ass"umer

That person who scowled at you and gave you a dirty look? They were actually squinting at the sign behind you.

That person who cut you off at the intersection? His wife is in labor, and he's rushing to the hospital.

That boy who was rude to you today? His mom and dad told him about their divorce last night.

That girl who talked behind your back and made up lies about you? She has suffered years of abuse at home from her mother.

That grumpy old man you always see frowning at the end of the street? He lost his wife and is still mourning the loss.

That young man who stole from your backpack? He hasn't eaten in three days and was searching for food.

Stop jumping to conclusions. You have no idea what people are going through. Assuming does not get you far in life. Choosing to assume only makes an "ass" out of "u" and "me."

Choose to see the good in everyone, and your life will be so much better. You will glow; you will be vibrant with life!

VERSE: Proverbs 3:7-9 "Don't assume that you know it all. Run to God! Run from evil! Your body will glow with health; your very bones will vibrate with life! Honor God with everything you own; give him the first and the best."

see the light

A camp I recently attended with some kids from my church had a day where we went on a canoe trip followed by a campout. We were pretty far away from the central camp and there was no cell phone service. It began to storm as it got dark, and soon rain and hail was coming down on the kids as well as thunder and lightning. We later found out there were tornado and flash flood warnings.

Three other counselors and I rushed them to a storm shelter where we waited for the storm to pass. We had no way to get radar nor had we any way to contact the people who could pick us up.

Despite the horrible situation, we played games, we laughed, we sang, we talked about Jesus, we prayed, and we made light of the situation. When we went back out to our tents, it began to storm again and instead of moping or becoming afraid, we stayed up super late laughing, making jokes, creating a rap about our situation, and quoting SpongeBob.

We laughed and laughed and laughed.

Although it was a dangerous, scary situation, we made the most of it. We learned from it, and we grew together.

Realize that not all the lessons in life come from great circumstances. Sometimes you must endure tough times to really open your eyes and discover something new.

Choose to see the light no matter what.

VERSE: Isaiah 43:1-3 "Do not fear, for I have redeemed you; I have called you by name, you are mine. When you pass through the waters, I will be with you; and through the rivers, they shall not overwhelm you; when you walk through fire you shall not be burned, and the flame shall not consume you. For I am the Lord Your God, the Holy One of Israel, your Savior."

abounding surrounding

I think people often overlook the power and influence others can have on them. Without you even realizing, the people you associate yourself with often start to become those you begin to reflect.

When you surround yourself with people who uplift you, people who challenge you in good ways, people who see all your great qualities and bring them to light, and people who always make sure you're giving your best, you will begin to live more positively and meaningfully.

Some things in life do not allow you a choice. But you normally can choose who you are around.

Make sure you choose wisely. Forgive and let go of those that hold you back.

VERSE: Proverbs 13:20 "Walk with the wise and become wise, for a companion of fools suffers harm."

strengthened by setbacks

A setback is defined as "a reversal or check in progress."

Sometimes God is going to throw obstacles your way. These obstacles are not meant to stump you or set you back.

They are there to make you stronger. They are meant to shape you into who God wants you to be.

Do not be discouraged.

What may not make sense now will someday be understood perfectly.

Know that God has a plan always.

VERSE: Romans 8:17-18 "Now if we are children, then we are heirs – heirs of God and coheirs with Christ, if indeed we share in His sufferings in order that we may also share in His glory. I consider that our present sufferings are not worth comparing with the glory that will be revealed in us."

justin bieber and the present

It's very easy to get stuck in a negative mindset when something doesn't go our way.

And even when something good does happen, we often still keep our minds on the things that were not so good.

I thought of this as I was listening to the radio. I was shuffling through stations, and as I was flipping through, I heard my jam come on that I was waiting and waiting to listen to. I started listening and then realized that the song was almost over. I was mad at myself for not discovering the station sooner, because I had been waiting to jam out like no other to that song.

Instead of enjoying the bit of the song that was left, I chose to mope about how I had missed a lot of it. I was too focused on what was missing rather than what I had at the moment.

Although this is a super miniscule example, I think changing an attitude with the little things in life like that really make a difference in the long run. Quit being so focused on what is not present or "not good enough" in your life, and make the choice to enjoy what you do have.

Even if it is only the end of Justin Bieber's new song.

VERSE: James 1:17 "Every good gift and every perfect gift is from above, coming down from the Father of lights with whom there is no variation or shadow due to change."

watch the 'tude

So much of the outcome of your day revolves around your attitude.

You can have the worst day, yet still have a positive attitude and your day suddenly will not be so bad.

You can choose to be frustrated by a friend or partner.

You can get high expectations set in your head of what you want your days to look like, of how you want people to treat you, of the accomplishments you think you must achieve in order to feel fulfilled.

Let go of that.
Let go of all the pressure and stress you put on yourself and others. Choose to simply accept.

Accept what happens to you, accept what obstacles arise and work to overcome them, accept what people do or say to you, because you are always being moved forward. Don't get stuck in an unhappy, what-if mindset.

Quit getting so frustrated.

Earn small victories by choosing to have a positive mindset no matter the circumstance. Watch your life begin to change.

VERSE: Psalm 118:24 "Today is the day the Lord has made; let us rejoice and be glad in it."

it's gon' get better

At some point in life you've got to understand that the world does not revolve around you.

You are special, but you are not what makes the world go round.

The best thing you can do in life is find what you love, pursue it, and inspire others to do the same. Leave each place you go better than you found it.

All the bad things in life are going to pass.
Things are going to get better.

But just remember that inconveniences and unfortunate circumstances don't mean you have a sucky life. They don't mean you're having a bad day. They don't mean people should feel sorry for you or that you have it worse than others.

Remember that there are other people in this world fighting similar or even worse battles.

Be an inspiration.
Find what you love.
Pursue it.
Inspire others to do the same.

VERSE: Isaiah 26:3 "You will keep in perfect peace those whose minds are steadfast, because they trust in You."

speeding tickets

So today I got up and was feeling pretty well rested. I looked at my phone. The verdict: 8:40 a.m.

I was supposed to be at work at 7:20 a.m.

I quickly got ready and made my way to work. One turn away from getting there, and I see the lights in my rearview mirror.

A cop pulls me over for speeding.

I'm tearing up as I stutter out my dilemma to him. I sit in the car and let the tears flow as I begin to think about paying for this ticket I was about to get... and explaining to my boss how I was two hours late. Yeah I know, I'm a baby. But the officer came back and gave me a warning. Boy, was I relieved. Getting a ticket would have been much worse, but it was still a rough morning.

Instead of letting it affect me the rest of the day, I decided to turn it around. I kept a positive attitude, and by the end of the day, a smile was stuck to my face. So yeah, everyone has bad circumstances. But don't let the bad circumstances turn into bad days, and don't let the bad days turn into bad attitudes.

Smile. Set three alarms. Slow down.

Life can be pretty darn good if you allow it to be.

VERSE: Ephesians 5:15-16 "Be very careful, then, how you live… making the most of every opportunity."

smile and shine

When you choose to be positive, you choose to accept the peace God is offering you. Those who choose to experience God's peace through their relationship with Him can have peace even in the midst of life's toughest storms.

If God has called you to do something, you will find yourself loving it despite any adversity you may face. What you think about is what you act upon.

Think of the right things.

Smile. You are far too beautiful to let negativity dull your sparkle.

Today you will shine.

VERSE: John 16:33 "I have told you these things, so that in me you may have peace. In this world you will have trouble. But take heart! I have overcome the world."

mindful of the mind

Life begins to change when we focus our minds on the right things.

When we focus on the good instead of the bad, when we be thankful instead of wishful, when we bring out the gifts and talents in others rather than flaws and faults, our lives become a little brighter, and we begin to shine even more.

When you begin to train your mind to be fixed on the good things, the small "bad" things begin to become less of a problem. We often like to make things worse than what they actually are. When a nice thought comes to mind, begin to communicate it.

A simple compliment can turn a day around.
Reflect on the good. Let go of the bad.

VERSE: Philippians 4:8 "Finally, brothers and sisters, whatever is true, whatever is noble, whatever is right, whatever is pure, whatever is lovely, whatever is admirable – if anything is excellent or praiseworthy – think about such things."

be the sunshine

"If you don't have anything nice to say, don't say anything at all."

Time and time again I have heard this, but I never actually understood how powerful this act of refraining from negativity could be until I put it into practice.

If someone does something I don't like or if something doesn't go my way, I can make it ten times worse by complaining to someone about it or expressing my temporary frustrations through attitude or grumbles.

When you begin to take away those verbal frustrations to people and quit talking so much smack, you begin to feel the difference in your attitude and well-being. Whenever I let something bad about someone slip out of my mouth, I immediately feel regret and guilt for releasing something so negative and unnecessary in the world.

Unkind words only bring darkness where there is light, they bring coldness where there is warmth, they bring storms where there is sunshine. Choose to be the light, warm, sunshine, and train your mind to rid itself of the negative set of mind.

VERSE: Proverbs 16:24 "Kind words are like honey – sweet to the soul and healthy for the body."

meant to be content

"I have learned the secret of being content in any and every situation, whether well fed or hungry, whether living in plenty or in want. I can do all this through him who gives me strength."

This is coming from a man in the Bible who was in prison awaiting false charges that could lead to execution due to corrupt officials.

Now this is a man who learned to be content in whatever situation he was in.

Today we are always looking after the next best thing. We believe products will fulfill our needs and looks; we are always on the move, looking for the next best house, the next best job, the next best car, the next best partner.

Oftentimes we see things we want, and we become consumed with how it would feel to attain such a thing. Realistically, the prior thoughts are often times more fulfilling and joyous than the actual attainment of what it is we want. And no matter how much we have this push to always reach for more, we are never satisfied.

The only thing that can fulfill us and fully satisfy us is God. Seeking after Him wholeheartedly and striving to have the best relationship with Him is what will bring fulfillment to our lives.

VERSE: Philippians 4:12-13 "I have learned the secret of being content in any and every situation, whether well fed or hungry, whether living in plenty or in want. I can do all this through him who gives me strength."

self-made problems

It's easy in life to think of the worst outcomes. It's easy to brace ourselves for bad things to happen. It's also easy to play out scenarios in our heads that aren't really real.

A close friend once brought to my attention that I create "self-made problems."

At first I was offended by this, but as I thought about it, he was absolutely right.

I was creating problems that didn't even exist and trying to come up with solutions to them in my head. My mind was over-thinking and creating problems before they were even a thing! Thinking how often my problems are "self-made" really put into perspective how much stress comes from my own self.

Have faith; have trust. Don't self-make your own problems.

Understand that tomorrow's answers usually don't appear until tomorrow.

Let go of all the negative possibilities or assumptions, and brace yourself for the best.

Enjoy life, and live in the now.

VERSE: Proverbs 4:20-27 "My son, pay attention to what I say; turn your ear to my words. Do not let them out of your sight, keep them within your heart; for they are life to those who find them and health to one's whole body. Above all else, guard your heart, for everything you do flows from it. Keep your mouth free of perversity; keep corrupt talk far from your lips. Let your eyes look straight ahead; fix your gaze directly before you. Give careful thought to the paths for your feet and be steadfast in all your ways. Do not turn to the right or the left; keep your foot from evil."

steady and stable

Being stable is so important in life but often not thought about.

Oftentimes we let our emotions get the best of us. We overreact and often fear the worst scenarios. When we allow our emotions to lead us, we are unstable and lost.

If Jesus allowed His emotions to overtake and guide Him while He was hanging on the cross or when He was being mocked and ridiculed throughout His life, do you think He would have responded with the same attitude and demeanor? Absolutely not.

Rather, He allowed the Holy Spirit to lead and balance Him. Jesus had emotions like we did. He *grieved, sobbed, groaned, wept,* was *surprised, amazed, full of joy, deeply moved, distressed, angry, sorrowful,* and He *desired* and *loved.* Emotions will happen, but we must learn to not let them overtake us. We must learn how to confide in God.

Manage your emotions.

You have a God that is consistent and steady. Lean on Him for the stability you need.

VERSE: Hebrews 13:8 "Jesus Christ is the same, yesterday, today, and forever."

dam right

The problem with today is everyone wants the next best thing: a better relationship, a better job, better friends, a better financial situation. Everyone's always comparing.

Think of a dam.
A dam is a barrier constructed to control the flow of water. It has to restrict the water level until the adequate amount of water is attained.

God is like our dam.

He places the right people, the right situations, the right experiences in our lives to set us in the right direction. And just when we feel we think we are filled to the brim, God opens the gates and makes everything new.

Quit trying to wish you have more or have less. God's got the perfect amount for you.

Trust Him.
Start being dam grateful.

VERSE: Luke 12:31 "Seek the kingdom of God above all else, and He will give you everything you need."

train the brain

You must learn to be content with whatever situation you are in. No matter the circumstance, learn to have a smile.

Worrying and wondering what would have happened had something gone differently is not going to change your outcome.

Embrace what life is giving you, and thank God for each new destination.

You're on a journey, and you've got to learn how to trust in the journey with blindness. Life throws you curve balls sometimes, but God will provide you with the right bat, the right coach, and the right swing so you can knock it out of the park.

Take a deep breath and learn to be content. Ask God to place love, happiness, and peace in your heart. God is far too great, life is far too short, and you are far too wonderful to let a "bad day" bring you down.

VERSE: Psalm 16:8-9 "I keep my eyes always on the Lord. With him at my right hand, I will not be shaken. Therefore, my heart is glad and my tongue rejoices; my body will also rest secure…"

watch your words

One thing I've really been trying to watch lately is my words.

Words are very powerful. They can bind, they can overcome, they can unite, but they can also destroy, they can break, they can hurt. That's why the use of them is so important.

If what you say is not helpful or lovely or uplifting or good or radiant, *don't say it*. Why dwell on and magnify negative things by speaking about them? Why spread that negativity and burden others with it?

When you speak, think about other people. Think about those who are opening their ears to you. Don't waste your breath or their time with unhelpful, negative words. If you are frustrated with someone, pray about them instead of talking bad about them. If a situation is not going how you want it to, do what you can to make it better and then let it go instead of complaining.

No matter how much you want to believe it, complaining about someone or something is not going to make anything better. Wishing for something else is not going to change your predicament.

Accept what is, let go of what holds you back, and let your words uplift and enlighten those around you.

VERSE: Ephesians 4:29 "Do not let any unwholesome talk come out of your mouths, but only what is helpful for building others up according to their needs, that it may benefit those who listen."

every day is yours

If you take your concerns to God in prayer and then go on and worry about them, there is a contradiction of your faith. Don't be the one to focus on the negatives and therefore miss the positives.

God is placing blessings in your life. Elevate these things.

Your trials and tribulations are meant to get you to a certain point. Instead of focusing on how far you have to go, focus on how far you have come and how far you are going. Instead of focusing on being half-empty, focus on being half-full.

Today is your day.

Every day is your day.

VERSE: John 14:26-27 "Peace I leave with you; my peace I give you. I do not give to you as the world gives. Do not let your hearts be troubled and do not be afraid."

radiance

1 pursue and pray
2 you do you
3 let go of the likes
4 pray away
5 be genuine
6 it will all fall away
7 razzle and dazzle
8 nothing for granted
9 like a child
10 slow your roll
11 make 'em feel it
12 humility
13 go for it
14 science and smiles
15 can't take it with you
16 brothers and sisters
17 be happy
18 normal is boring
19 pray
20 beams of light
21 made to shine

pursue and pray

You never know whose life you could be impacting. You just really never know who is looking up to you.

You will find that God works in pretty mysterious ways sometimes.

I have been praying and praying to God for Him to help me radiate light in this world. I have kept asking Him to give me a light that others can see, a light that brightens other people's days.

I posted a picture recently of myself outside surrounded by beautiful nature with me beaming up at the sky looking to God. I captioned it "Follow His light." The next day as I was sitting at the table, my mom told me that someone I used to know pretty well saw my mom at the grocery store, went up to her, and said with tearful eyes, "I opened up Facebook this morning, and Madison's picture popped up, and it was such a light in my day. It made me so happy. I needed to see that today, and I'm so happy she provided that light."

I just thought how awesome it was that I had been praying and praying about this very thing. I had no idea something so small could light up someone's day. It just goes to show that even the smallest of things can go a long way for someone. It also shows that God knows what's best and hears our prayers.

Don't let fear or intimidation keep you from reaching out to someone or pursuing what you really want in life.

Keep praying.

Understand that even the smallest of choices along your journey can serve as motivation for others along theirs.

VERSE: Luke 16:10 "Unless you are faithful in small matters, you won't be faithful in large ones."

you do you

I hope by now in life you have realized that there is someone out there faster than you. There is someone out there stronger than you. There is someone out there who is smarter, has nicer hair, who is funnier.

But none of this – I repeat – none of this matters.

There are people in life who may be better than you at certain things. But no one is better than you at being you.

So own that.

Quit trying to compete with other people, always sizing yourself up to what they have, to what they can do, to what they have done.

You don't have to be the best to shine the brightest.

Live at peace with who you are, and let your light shine without allowing it to be dimmed by others. Do not think you are not enough just because someone can outdo you in a certain department.

It is not your job, nor anybody's job, to compare people. Everybody has their own purpose; everybody has their own strengths, their own fears, their own dreams.

Let them be. You do you.

VERSES: 1 Corinthians 12:4-6 "There are different kinds of gifts, but the same Spirit distributes them. There are different kinds of service, but the same Lord. There are different kinds of working, but in all of them and in everyone it is the same God at work."

1 Corinthians 12:12 "Just as a body, though one, has many parts, but all its many parts form one body, so it is with Christ."

let go of the likes

We give too much control over to the people around us.

We think too much about how people will respond to us, what they will say about our actions, what they will do toward our expressed words, or how they will feel about us as individuals.

Please, please, please make it easier on yourself and learn not to take everything so seriously.

It is not your job to please people.

The greatness of life is not measured by how many people like us. It is about how many people we have impacted; how many people we have brought up along the way. Stop putting so much energy into getting approval and "likes" from other people.

We too often base our acceptance on how many people like our Instagram posts or how many friends we have on Facebook. Do not give so much control over to a finger either clicking a button or not clicking it.

Likes do not signify you as an automatic awesome person. Quit putting so much energy into pleasing. Start shining by being yourself and getting others to shine along with you.

VERSE: 1 John 2:15-17 "Do not love the world or the things in the world. If anyone loves the world, the love of the Father is not in him. For all that is in the world – the desires of the flesh and the desires of the eyes and pride in possessions – is not from the Father but is from the world. And the world is passing away along with its desires, but whoever does the will of God abides forever."

pray away

Life gets pretty busy. Places to be, things to see, people to meet.

Sometimes people can forget to even breathe.

With the hustle and bustle of life, it's important to take the time to understand others and pray for them.

Life isn't all about you. Life is about reaching out to others and serving them.

And prayer.
Prayer is so powerful.

Oftentimes we get into a habit of talking to God about our troubles, our wants in life, our unfortunate circumstances etc. And in the midst of that, we forget to think of others in either very similar situations or oftentimes even more difficult ones.

Pray for other people.

It could make all the difference in the world for someone if you take a little time and offer a little piece of yourself, some energy, and your heart for them.

Do this very thing, and you will begin to see yourself radiate light even more.

VERSE: Ephesians 6:18 "And pray in the Spirit on all occasions with all kinds of prayers and requests. With this in mind, be alert and always keep on praying for all the Lord's people."

be genuine

Don't hold back compliments.

When you start to look for the good in others, you begin to see the good in yourself.

Have you ever been given a compliment that made your whole day? You could be the one to make someone's day every single day of your life if you wanted to.

If you have something nice to say, absolutely say it.
You never know who is needing to hear a nice compliment.

Be genuine.

Don't tell people what you think they want to hear. Tell them genuine thoughts you have. People will respect you for bringing the good out and will love you all the more for it. You will be in a better mood and will enjoy life more if you choose to see the good in the world.

VERSE: Matthew 5:16 "In the same way, let your light shine before others, so that they may see your good works and give glory to your Father who is in heaven."

it will all fall away

Death is such a strange thing.

It's something everyone must go through. It's something that fills some people with fear. Death is a part of life.

Imagine this: your last day is tomorrow.
Your last day here on this earth is tomorrow.

Would all the little things you're worried and wondering about this instant really matter if you were to be gone tomorrow? Would you put so much of your emotions into what that girl said about you or into the man who cut you off on the intersection or the busy, stressful day at work you had? Would you go through lists and lists of things to do and get done? Would you worry about who likes you or who approves of you? Would you groan and complain about everything that's going on in your life?

I'd like to say you wouldn't if tomorrow was your last day.

Don't get so caught up in getting by in life and receiving acceptance that you forget to actually love, enjoy, and fully embrace it. With death, everything else falls away. All glamour, all pride, all embarrassment, all expectations, all fears or failures. None of that matters.

Love like crazy, fully embrace, and follow your heart.
Everything else will fall into place.

VERSE: Mark 8:34-35 "And calling the crowd to him with his disciples, he said to them, 'If anyone would come after me, let him deny himself and take up his cross and follow me. For whoever would save his life will lose it, but whoever loses his life for my sake and the gospel's will save it.'"

razzle and dazzle

Sometimes inner beauty is overlooked by the world, but never for God. He has given you a shine, a radiance.

He has created you to be brilliant. He has created you to be light.

Even what the world looks at and says is beautiful can be dulled by a lack of radiance. You are not lacking in that area.

You are radiant. You are irresistible. You are brilliant.

Let the light shine that He has instilled in you. Glow when you walk into a room. Dazzle with your brilliance. Choosing to embrace this inner beauty is far more powerful than any physical and exterior quality.

VERSE: Ephesians 5:8 "For at one time you were darkness, but now you are light in the Lord. Walk as children of light."

nothing for granted

Don't take anything for granted.

What you have now could be gone tomorrow.

Give thanks.
Show your appreciation.
Stay energized.
Remain aware.
Keep praying.
Always love.

You have been given talents and abilities – don't take them for granted. Use them. Serve others with them. Give back happily to those who need it… you never know when you might be in that position.

You have been given wonderful people and opportunities – don't take them for granted. Every day is a gift. Life is a blessing. Embrace each day with thankfulness, goodness, kindness, and lovely, lovely thoughts.

VERSE: 1 Peter 4:7-11 "The end of all things is near. Therefore, be alert and of sober mind so that you may pray. Above all, love each other deeply, because love covers over a multitude of sins. Offer hospitality to one another without grumbling. Each of you should use whatever gift you have received to serve others, as faithful stewards of God's grace in its various forms. If anyone speaks, they should do so as one who speaks the very words of God. If anyone serves, they should do so with the strength God provides, so that in all things God may be praised through Jesus Christ. To Him be the glory and the power for ever and ever."

like a child

The other day I saw a photo album laying out from when I was around seven years old. I opened it up and started going through it.

Wow, I was such a happy child.

There was rarely a picture where I wasn't smiling or making a funny face. I knew exactly who I was and with all my crazy, multiple interests, I was happy and radiant.

Growing up and getting older came with pressure and questions. It came with figuring out who I was, how I related to those around me, how I best fit into the world.

Little did I know that the seven-year-old me had it all figured out to begin with.

Children are so darn smart. Jesus even talks in the Bible about being like a child.

Children don't have to worry.

They don't have to think and wonder about who they are –
they just know.
They don't have to worry about impressing people –
they do what makes them happy.
They pursue all their passions and desires –
despite the odds against them.

When I start to feel the weight of the world and all the influences that come along with it, I always ask myself what the little Madison would do. That answer guides me to living the life I truly want to live, not the life the world is telling me to live.

Don't be afraid to think like a child.
Learn from them. Grow with them. Dream like them.

VERSE: Matthew 18:3 "And he said, 'Truly I tell you, unless you change and become like little children, you will never enter the kingdom of heaven.'"

146

slow your roll

It's very easy in this life to go 100 mph. So many things to get done, so many places to be, so many things to see.

It's important to take the time to slow down and take a breath. It's important to your health.

Stop and breathe.
Put God first instead.

There's enough going on in life as it is. Don't add to the chaos by speeding through life. It seems that the faster we live, the less emotions we feel in this world. The slower we live, the deeper we live.

Slow down. Live deeply.
Live for Jesus.

VERSE: 1 John 2:17 "The world and its desires pass away, but whoever does the will of God lives forever."

make 'em feel it

You may ask, "Father, how am I radiant? How am I brilliant? How do I dazzle?"

The answer is being yourself, not a replica of someone else.

Be passionate, discover the joys God has instilled in you, and pursue them with your whole heart.

Be genuine, want the best for others rather than just looking after yourself.

Smile, laugh, tell your little jokes.
Run, jump, express all of who you are.
Be brave, be bold, be daring.

People may forget what you said, people may forget what you did, but people will never forget how you made them feel.

Let them feel your radiance.

VERSE: Ephesians 5:19-20 "Sing and make music from your heart to the Lord, always giving thanks to God the Father for everything, in the name of our Lord Jesus Christ."

humility

When you feel yourself shining, when you can feel your beams of light touching other people, be humble about it.

When the Bible talks about humility, it makes sure to mention how you should treat and think about others. The best way to be humble is to put other people before yourself.

It is to be selfless.

Being selfish leads to arrogance and pride. It leads to thinking you are better than others. Don't let comparisons and conceit rule your mind and attitude. You will not always be on top. Be happy in whatever situation you are in.

Accept advice from others. Let go of the idea that you are always right. Understand when it is time to apologize. Never stop showing respect.

When good things go your way, be happy.
There is no need to brag.
When you accomplish things in life, be thankful.
There is no need to boast.
When opportunities arise, be grateful.
There is no need to compare.

You don't need to wave your own light around.
Your light will shine the way it should.

VERSE: 2 Corinthians 8:7 "But as you excel in everything – in faith, in speech, in knowledge, in all earnestness, and in our love for you – see that you excel in this act of grace also."

go for it

Bringing out the best in others multiplies your light a thousand times over. If you feel an urge to give someone a compliment or say something nice about them DO IT. You never know how much of an impact you can have on someone just by saying one nice thing.

Oftentimes we have ideas in our heads but we keep things bottled. We don't share our insights with the world out of fear they might be rejected or responded to negatively.

I'm telling you now: GO FOR IT. You have nothing to lose. Radiance has so much to do with how you treat people.

Share the love.

VERSE: Ephesians 5:1 "Therefore be imitators of God, as beloved children. And walk in love, as Christ loved us and gave himself up for us, a fragrant offering and sacrifice to God."

science and smiles

Have you ever smiled at a baby and saw them smile right back? Try it out.

It is because smiles are contagious – it's a proven scientific fact. Neuropeptides allow molecules to communicate things like messages that say when we are happy, sad, angry, depressed, and excited.

Dopamine, endorphins, and serotonin are feel good neurotransmitters that all get released when we smile. This relaxes our bodies and lowers our heart rate and blood pressure.

The cingulate cortex of our brain is responsible for the facial expressions of smiling when happy or copying another person's smile. So if people are not smiling back at you, it is because they are making a conscious effort not to.

In other words, start smiling.
Others will too.

VERSE: Proverbs 15:30 "A cheerful look brings joy to the heart; good news makes for good health."

can't take it with you

Sometimes in life I've got to sit back and ask myself, "When I leave this earth, is this very thing going to matter?"

I've got to remind myself that I will not be able to take anything with me when I go.

All I will leave behind is how much I loved, how I made people feel, and what I gave back to all those around me.

All the likes and followers in the world won't come with me when I pass, all the high dollar shoes and clothes I bought won't join me, the stupid question I missed on that test won't matter, and all the disappointments I had to experience will be a thing of the past.

What will matter is the kind of impact I make.
What will matter is how I treat people.
What will matter is how I love.
What will matter is how I choose to uplift and be a light to the world.
What will matter is whether or not I used every ounce of talent God has instilled within me.

Let go of all the little things in life, and just live.
Leave your mark, and let go of approval or material things.

Love, create, uplift, let go, be light.

VERSE: Colossians 2:6-7 "And now, just as you accepted Christ Jesus as your Lord, you must continue to follow Him. Let your roots grow down into Him, and let your lives be built on Him. Then your faith will grow strong in the truth you were taught, and you will overflow with thankfulness."

brothers and sisters

There is something so uniquely radiant about an individual who wants the absolute best for others.

Your goal should be to bring the best out in people. You should strive to help others see their light.

The best thing you can do is to get the people in front of you to shine.

Sometimes we get stuck in comparisons and jealousy. We don't view others as our brothers and sisters. We strive to be at the top, and on our journey we forget to bring others along with us.

Radiance doesn't just mean making yourself shine – it's about shedding light on others and bringing out the absolute best in others.

God wants us to love each other. He sees how much each one of us has to offer, and He desires for us to bring that potential out in one another.

VERSE: Romans 12:10 "Be devoted to one another in brotherly love; give preference to one another in honor."

be happy

Wilhelm von Humboldt once said, "Our happiness or our unhappiness depends far more on the way we meet the events of life than on the nature of those events themselves."

Radiance and happiness go hand in hand. When you choose to be happy with you are, with what you have, and with what happens to you, you will become a light.

That light will shine for others, and it will be recognizable to those you come into contact with.

Sure, you can mope about that bad haircut or be angry someone ate the last brownie, but being mad and unhappy isn't going to change your circumstances.

Accept whatever it is that has happened to you, see the good in the situation, and happily move forward.

Your hair will grow back, and brownies aren't good for you anyways, right?

Keep smiling. Keep shining. Never let the world keep you down.

VERSE: Philippians 4:19 "And my God will meet all your needs according to the riches of his glory in Christ Jesus."

normal is boring

If you want to stand out, you have to do something different. You can't do what everyone else is doing.

You have to be uncomfortable.

Did Helen Keller become well-known by moping about her disabilities? No, she overcame both deafness and blindness and helped improve society's treatment of deaf and blind people.

Did Moses become well-known by following his masters as a slave? No, he escaped slavery in Egypt and led his people out of Egypt and across the Red Sea.

Did Thomas Jefferson become well-known by watching his peers write the Declaration of Independence? No, he challenged the existing policies on religious tolerance, education, and slavery and was the foremost author of the Declaration of Independence.

Did Martin Luther King Jr. become well-known by accepting his fate at the time? No, he fought against racial discrimination and supported the civil rights movement – despite all opposition and discrimination.

Did Rosa Parks become well-known by listening and moving to the back of the bus? No, she refused to give up her seat and started a mass protest resulting in an end to segregation on public transport.

Did Jesus Christ keep quiet and grow up a normal boy? No, he stuck to the truth of His Message, never wavering from it. He challenged people. He suffered outer humiliation, pain, and ultimately death in order to leave a legacy of spiritual truth.

Do you want to stand out? Do something different.

VERSE: 1 Peter 4:10-11 "God has given each of you a gift from his great variety of spiritual gifts. Use them well to serve one another. Do you have the gift of speaking? Then speak as though God himself were speaking through you. Do you have the gift of helping others? Do it with all the strengths and energy that God supplies. Then everything you do will bring glory to God through Jesus Christ."

pray

Prayer.
Oh my goodness, prayer.

It's hard to wrap your mind around how powerful it is.

There have been times where I just feel low. I have felt as though something was attacking my emotions, my thoughts, my mind, and my confidence. The devil tries to sneak his way in however he possibly can, and he will use anything to make you believe his lies.

I'm telling you now: pray.
Pray, pray, pray.
Just like in life, if you don't ask, you probably won't receive.

Ask God for strength, for deliverance, for guidance. Pray for the right mindset, for positivity, for an uplifting attitude.

Use the power of prayer to shake off the devil. He normally attacks when he knows you are about to move mountains.

You've got such big things in store.

Don't let the world or your own thoughts keep you from moving those mountains.

Pray.
About everything.

Watch your life become more radiant, peaceful, uplifting, and powerful. Amen.

VERSE: Jeremiah 33:3 "Call to me and I will answer you and tell you great and unsearchable things you do not know."

beams of light

I recently attended a church camp where I took a group of students from my church for the week. For a while before this, I had been praying that I would be light in the world. I had been asking God that He would allow me to shine and be light.

One night during camp, we were having a campfire and praying with one another.

A little boy I had just met that night came up to me and sweetly asked, "Could I please pray with you? I'm trying to pray with as many people as possible."

Of course I went off to pray with him, and when it was his turn he had his arm around me and he said, "Dear Father, thank you for bringing Madison into my life today and for this blessed adventure. When I look at Madison and all around her, I just see these radiant beams of light. When I look in her eyes, I just see pure joy. I can see You working within her. Thank you for these beautiful minutes and moments with Madison. Amen."

Boy, did I tear up. What an awesome answer from God.

Something so specific I had been asking for was acknowledged by a little boy I had just met.

Talk about powerful.

I will ask God for my light to be shown every day that I live my life, for I know that He is working within me always, allowing me to shine. And He will do the same for you.

VERSE: 1 John 5:14-15 "This is the confidence we have in approaching God: that if we ask anything according to His will, He hears us. And if we know that He hears us – whatever we ask – we know that we have what we asked of Him."

made to shine

Stop worrying and enjoy life.

You don't have to feel this way. This worrying, this overthinking. This stress is only weighing you down. This moment won't matter years down the road.

Quit getting so caught up in overanalyzing every situation that you forget to enjoy this moment. You have accomplished so much and have inspired so many people.

Pay attention to the condition of your mind and keep it free, peaceful, and full of faith.

Look around and enjoy life. Stop worrying. Trust. Forgive. Love. Embrace. Live life to the fullest. Be happy.

You deserve it.

If you get hurt that's not your fault. God is placing the things in your life you need and taking the things out you don't.

Love and be happy.

You get one life to live – don't waste it worrying. Don't dull your own sparkle. Be radiant and start beaming.

Shine and enjoy. Love life.

VERSE: Psalm 37:4 "Delight yourself in the Lord, and He will give you the desires of your heart."

about the author

MADISON BLOKER

Starting at the age of thirteen, Madison Bloker has kept a journal of her life. Each night she writes to God to thank Him for the day, talk about what she learned and did, and release any worries or thoughts she has. Whether big moments or small ones, she's got them documented. Madison also writes to her siblings each day. Her love of writing and faith has pushed her to write this book. She aims to inspire, uplift, and enlighten. You can read more of her writings at www.boundblessings.com where she transparently discusses her faith and life journey and shares the stories of many others.